When Souls Commune:

Creating Authentic Connections

Gary Michael

Talk Doc Books

Denver, Colorado

When Souls Commune: Creating Authentic Connections

Copyright ©2001 by Gary Michael

Published by

Talk Doc Books

3009 E. 10th Avenue

Denver, CO 80206

303-321-6607

talkdoc@ecentral.com

ISBN 0-9655295-8-4

Cover art by Madeline Wiener—"And Two Shall Become As One"

Cover design and book layout by Nick Zelinger, NZ Graphics, Lakewood, CO

Conceptual Editing by Erika Niemann, Close Connections Publishing, Evergreen, CO

Printed by Little Booklets & Manuals, Evergreen, CO

For DeAnne, my friend and ally,
with abiding love

Thanks...

To John Haien, Dave Betz, Perry Fisher, and Robert Hale for suggestions on different parts of the manuscript, and Erika Niemann for her patient editing and firm encouragement. They helped make the book possible. To all who have attended one of my talks, classes or seminars—they made the book necessary. And to friends and adversaries, past and present, who have made me see myself through their eyes, thus enlarging my vision, I pray to my betterment.

Table Of Contents

"At the center of our being is a point of nothingness...untouched by sin and by illusion, a point of pure truth...which belongs entirely to God.... (It) is inaccessible to the fantasies of our own mind or the brutalities of our own will. This little point of nothingness...is the pure glory of God in us.... It is in everybody, and if we could see it we would see these billions of points of light coming together in the face and blaze of a sun, which would make all the darkness and cruelty of life vanish completely. I have no program for this seeing. It is only given. But the gate of heaven is everywhere."

– Thomas Merton

An Unpromising Beginning

I was so shy as a kid I could not have led my class in silent prayer. Instead of fading with age, the shyness increased. As an adolescent, I had no social skills, felt rejected by my peers, and was afraid to ask a girl out. When I lettered in track in high school, my self-esteem improved to the point I could make conversation, even dates, with girls I already knew. The thought of approaching a strange woman terrified me. I didn't know what I could say that wouldn't sound either stilted or stupid. Any rejection wounded me.

My fear led to self-loathing. In addition to the "chicken" complex I had because I was afraid to try risky athletic endeavors, like pole vaulting or playing catcher in schoolyard baseball games, I now regarded myself as a social coward. Eventually my self-disgust became so severe I vowed to overcome my paralysis. So I grew a moustache, got a fake I.D., and started going to honkytonks—alone.

At first, it took all my meager courage to ask women to dance. Most accepted, and the activity of dancing made it easier for me to talk, if asking what a woman's name is can be considered talking. This project revealed that even if a woman declined to dance with me, I could withstand this affront to my manhood.

Thus began a personal social odyssey that led not only to an ability to initiate conversations with strangers, but an eagerness to do so. I've made good friends with people I'd never have known had I not just started talking to them, whether at a party, play, or park. Even when an encounter has been fleeting, as in a bus or on a plane, the interactions have nourished me. Connection need not prove lasting to assuage the soul. Sometimes a brief meeting can fortify you with a sense of having touched and been touched at a deep level.

Less than a week after emergency surgery to repair a ruptured tendon in my knee, I boarded a crowded New York City bus. A woman, who saw how difficult my splinted leg made any movement, much less getting on and off a bus, asked what had happened. When I told her, she was incredulous that I subjected myself to air travel to hobble around Manhattan. "It beats sitting home feeling sorry for myself," I told her.

During our short visit she told me she'd had stomach surgery three years earlier and since then, for fear of recurrent problems, kept postponing a planned trip to Egypt. When I told her goodbye as I got up to work my way to the door, she said, "Thank you."

"For what?" I asked.

"For inspiring me to quit worrying about myself and go to Egypt. I'll do it this year!"

PART ONE

A Fantastic First Impression

O nce upon a time, to make a good first impression you thought you had to let other people know how important you were. Of course you couldn't be blatant about it; braggarts make terrible impressions, first or last. The idea was to wait until the conversation got to a point where you could mention— very off-handedly—that you lettered in three sports, dated the prom queen, or drove a convertible. The subtler you said it, the better. Any gesture, vocal inflection, or facial expression that portrayed pride defeated your purpose.

That was a long time ago. The so-called Sensitivity Movement of the late Sixties and early Seventies changed things. Building other people up instead of yourself became the norm. Revealing your vulnerability made you more real than trying to make yourself appear invulnerable. Timothy Leary, an ex-Harvard professor, coined the catch phrase, "Turn on, tune in, drop out." The "tune in" part meant to become more aware of yourself and others. Your sensitivity and capacity for feeling, not your status in the conventional sense, determined your merit as a human being.

When Robert Thurman, a personal friend of the Dalai Lama, spoke at a Denver bookstore, someone asked him, "What is the most important lesson you learned from the Dalai Lama?" He responded: "To focus your attention on others instead of yourself."

Dr. Thurman's answer is the theme for much of this book.

Today a good first impression is about being more present for other people. By paying attention to, and showing interest in, the person in front of you, you make that person feel important. Show people you are not just pleased but very pleased to meet them and want to know more about them. The more important you can make another person feel, the more positive an impression you'll make.

What makes a good first impression is care, as demonstrated by presence. In the first part of this book we'll look at how to become more present for other people. In the second we'll explore how to be truer to them through authenticity.

Chapter One:
How To Greet People

Initial Contact

Most of us are a little lazy in our greetings. We treat a greeting as an obligatory social ritual that's a mere prelude to important interaction. What a mistake that is: First impressions begin with first contact. And first contact is almost always eye contact. We look at the person we're about to meet before we speak, smile, or shake hands. From the moment our eyes meet another's the first impression is underway. Actually it may have begun with the other person observing you without your having known it. Let's start with the all-important first moment of mutuality—when your eyes find each other's.

As soon as your eyes meet, use your whole body to express your eagerness to meet the person. Stand erect, move decisively, smile—anything you can to convey excitement. This will prove much more effective than waiting until you're right in front of someone, then turning on a smile when you extend a hand or say hello. How do you think it makes another person feel when you look eager to meet him or her? The same way it makes you feel when someone looks as though he or she can't wait to make your acquaintance—terrific.

One way to communicate enthusiasm for the imminent encounter is to act as though the other person is a dear friend whom you haven't seen for a long time. Or you can anticipate that he or she will soon become your dear friend. Either thought will get a big smile on your face, a gleam in your eye, and energy into your stride.

I remember fondly a first meeting of many years ago. A cashier in the corner grocery saw paint spatters on my clothes and asked if I was an artist. When I told her I was trying to become one, she offered to introduce me to the picture framer for whom she worked weekends. "Just show up at the shop Saturday afternoon."

As I approached the door that Saturday, I looked in the big window and saw, beaming at me, the owner. I thought, "This man doesn't even know me, probably thinks I'm one more artist looking for scrap frames, and he looks as though he can't wait to meet me. What a guy!" We've been friends ever since.

Shaking Hands

Next comes the handshake. We send lots of subtle messages in the simple act of shaking hands, sometimes ones we don't intend. The way you hold another person's hand can convey presence and enthusiasm or aloofness and disdain. Engage the other person's hand so that your thumb notch contacts his or hers. Anything less may say you don't really want to touch and even, that you find touch distasteful. Have a firm but not over-bearing grip. A wimpy grip runs the same risk as incomplete contact. Too much macho and you may hurt someone, never a good way to begin. Use the same squeeze for men and women but let up a little for older folks whose arthritis may make them more vulnerable to discomfort.

To communicate to the other person that he or she controls

the transaction — like someone you want to buy from or hire you – incline your palm upward slightly. The upturned palm signals the other person that he or she is in charge and need not feel threatened by you. Don't overdo it or you'll appear obsequious.

I was amazed at a business breakfast meeting when a man shook my hand by turning his palm way down. Everything else about him was likable. He smiled warmly, did not make the mistake of squeezing too hard, and looked pleased to meet me. Yet he created a strong negative impression by putting his hand on top of mine.

Maintain contact for at least two seconds. Too fleeting a shake comes across like a jab rather than presence. A two handed shake conveys greater intimacy. It works well with touchy-feely types like me but may put off the less tactile among us. Unless you've observed your target in advance and deem him or her a lover of touch, it's best to let the ancillary elbow grab or shoulder pat wait for a later encounter.

If you have a firm shake, it may presage a healthy old age. Researchers reported in the Journal of the American Medical Association that a 25-year study of more than 6,000 Japanese-American men living in Hawaii found handgrip strength at midlife was a powerful predictor of physical vitality in later years. Men with good grips stayed healthy longer.

Eye Contact

Note the person's eye color. In this way you create eye contact in a very natural, non-threatening way. Maintain the eye contact even after you've disengaged hands. One of the most common mistakes we make is to look toward other targets before we've established real rapport with the person in front of us. It has an effect like that of a receiver running with the football before he's caught it.

Eye contact is culture specific. Mainstream American culture values it as a sign of sincerity. We are suspicious of people who talk to us without looking at us. They appear more interested in what they are saying than the person they're supposedly talking to. The most egregious examples make us wonder if we are but a pretext for them to hold forth.

The same eye contact that makes a hit with most Americans can have the opposite effect in parts of Asia. Japanese people, in particular, have complex, status-oriented mores about who gives whom how much of it. In some Native American groups, if a youth looks at an elder when addressing him, it's a sign of disrespect.

I once interviewed for a teaching job at a local seminary. My answers to a variety of questions, both academic and philosophical, were good, I thought. Yet I had a sinking feeling afterward and realized I had failed to look at my interlocutor, the Dean of Faculty, when responding. Instead I delivered my answers to the ceiling and walls of his office, glancing at him occasionally to see if he was paying attention. "I don't deserve the job," I thought. The Dean must have agreed; he didn't hire me.

Facial Expression

Smile throughout the introduction. Nothing lubricates a dialogue like a smile. You want to look as though you're not just "pleased" but damn happy to meet the person. This makes him or her feel good and encourages conversation.

Not all smiles have equal weight. The full tooth smile flashed as though on cue will serve you less well than one developed slowly. The slower smile shows sincerity and developing appreciation for your partner. If you throw all you have into your smile too soon, you have nothing in reserve to register your delight at a surprise piece of information your partner may utter. Suppose you have a special fondness for Russian wolfhounds and your partner announces that he or she just got one. What a perfect place for the widest grin you can muster, accompanied by an energetic "Wow!"

It's a physiological fact that our pupils get larger when we hear what we like. By holding a good thought for the person you're talking to, you can make your pupils a little bigger. This translates to the person as pleasure in, even excitement at, his or her company. And when you send someone a positive thought, however silent, you make it easier for yourself to smile in a natural way.

I also recommend you keep your eyes open a little wider than you do in your neutral demeanor. It shows interest and alertness. When the other person finishes a statement, keep your eyes on him or her for another moment before replying. Remember to nod, both while the other person is speaking and when he or she finishes. This shows you've taken in the message and want to ponder it for a second before responding. It shows you have been listening carefully, not just waiting to talk. It will make a huge difference in other people's perception of your sincerity.

Body Language

Regard your whole body as a tool for communicating elation. Important as dress and grooming are, energy is even more so. An instant way to energize yourself and enhance your smile is to hold a positive thought. For example, "You have bright eyes," or "I hope you enjoy the meeting."

Stand straight, with shoulders back and chin high. Lean forward slightly when you address people. Erect posture connotes confidence. Leaning toward the other person makes you appear more present and happy about the meeting. If the other person then leans back, you may want to also, lest you come off as too eager. If he or she doesn't move either back or forward, it's a sign of comfort with your presence. If he or she reciprocates your forward lean, you know the interaction is off to a dynamite start.

Keep your body open to the person you're talking to. If you cross your arms in front of your chest, you close yourself off. When your hands are at your sides, turn your palms toward your partner. It connotes openness and accessibility. If instead of face-to-face, you stand at a slight angle to the person, you'll give him or her more personal space. You'll also appear more inviting to others who might like to join you.

When at a function featuring food, mingle first and munch later. Or reverse the order if you arrive famished. You can't both eat and be fully present for others at the same time, unless you sit down with someone who's also eating. Even then, pay more attention to the person than your plate. Remember the biblical observation that what comes out of your mouth is more important than what goes in.

Name Recall

Whether we admit it or not, everyone's favorite word is his or her name. To forget the name of the person we've just introduced ourselves to presents a dilemma. Do we suffer embarrassment by asking for the person's name, or try to bluff our way through and hope our lapse of memory goes unnoticed? When we remember a person's name, we've gone a long way toward making him or her feel important.

Like all skills, name recall is a matter of motivation, technique, and practice. Repeat a person's name as soon as you hear it. "Ron, I'm very pleased to meet you." Of the many techniques for name recall, repetition is best and easiest. So say the name again when you conclude the conversation. "Let's talk more later, Ron."

Association is another useful technique. Visualize a Bill, Bob, or Bonny you know standing with an arm around the Bill, Bob, or Bonny you've just met. You can also make up associations on the spot. For a Victoria, you can see her standing under a waterfall—Victoria Falls. For Tracy, see him or her wearing a police badge and yellow fedora—Dick Tracy. John could have a toilet seat around his neck.

The very best name-recall technique is concentration. Get in the habit of listening carefully when people say their names. Focus makes friends.

OK, you say, but sooner or later I'll forget a name. What then? Rather than continue the conversation as though you had not, admit what you did. If you're over fifty, you might say, "Oops, I just had a senior moment. Please tell me your name again." If under fifty, "Please forgive me. My hard drive just crashed. Will you repeat your name for me?" Or: "I may have to change my diet because my brain is leaking like a puppy's bladder. Give me your name again, please." Maybe best of all, just take accountability. "I'm sorry, I didn't register your name. Please tell me again." Then, "Thank you, ___."

Compliments

Find something on which you can give a sincere compliment. Behavior is best. "You have terrific posture, Ann. Were you born with it or did you work to develop it?" If you've observed a commendable sample of behavior on the other person's part, by all means reference it. "I saw how you held the door for that older man, Justin, and commend you for your kindness."

I went by myself on a diving trip to Cozumel. At every meal, I asked couples if I could join them at their table. On the last day of the trip, I asked a couple I'd not previously sat with. "Oh please do," said the lady with obvious pleasure. "I've noticed how gently you treat people, especially the waiters. You're so much more polite than the other Americans here." I was deeply touched by her observation and wanted to hug her.

If you can't compliment behavior, apparel will suffice. How we dress has less to do with character than how we behave, but a kind remark about our good taste is always welcome. Some of my favorite ways to phrase apparel compliments are:
1. "My compliments to your color coordinator."
2. "Congratulations. I give your outfit 'Best of Show'."
3. "What a cool suit. Please call me when you outgrow it."

An even more forceful way to put an apparel compliment to someone is: "Boy, you look good in that sweater." The addition of the "you" gives the compliment more impact, as does making it apply both to the apparel and the person.

You can also tack on a question. "What an interesting pin. Does it have a story behind it?" The question gives the person a chance to talk. Most people like telling stories about themselves, so make it easy for them by following a compliment with a question.

In telling their stories people reveal more about themselves—interests, fears, aspirations. Knowing something of these will help you create rapport down the road.

I met Marsha at a MENSA meeting. She wore an unusual pearl necklace. I complimented her on it and asked if had special meaning. This is what she told me.

"Fifteen years ago, a man named Glen and I were both in Eba's Boutique in Hawaii. No sooner did we make eye contact than sparks flew. Eba, owner of the store, saw the electric interaction and offered us her car so we could take a ride together. By the time we left Hawaii ten days later, our romance was in full flower. Even though Glen lived in San Francisco and I in Vancouver, we vowed to keep up the contact.

"Eight months of long distance love left me drained and disillusioned. I saw no future for myself with Glen. On the final night of one of his visits to Vancouver, I told him, "This is goodbye. I can't do it anymore." That night I got pregnant.

"I thought of getting an abortion, then remembered the last thing Eba had told me when I stopped by the boutique to say goodbye: 'If you get pregnant keep the baby.' I took the advice but stopped seeing Glen and lost touch with him.

"At age twelve, our son, Brian, said he wanted to meet his father. When I learned from Glen's company that he had moved to Denver and gotten an unlisted number, I got mad. I was out of work and had just left the man I'd been living with. Time has come, I thought, for Glen to take responsibility for Brian. The Canadian Court System tracked him down in Denver and threatened to exact $500 per month from his salary. Glen then called me and asked to negotiate. 'Come meet our son,' I told him. 'It's your turn to care for him.'

"Glen agreed to visit me and Brian in Vancouver. As I drove to the airport, I reflected on something else Eba had told me: 'Think nice things about Glen. When he stepped off the plane, I took one look and thought: 'Oh shit, he looks better than ever.' Desire reared its rowdy head but I demurred; I was already living with another man.

"Glen and Brian hit it off. Two months after Glen's visit to Vancouver, I called him and said, 'I'm getting my own place. It doesn't have room for two. Please come get Brian.' Glen obliged. When he dropped by to say goodbye, I made a request: 'Take me to bed.' Again Glen obliged. Then I said, 'Please leave now. You've just been used.' "From Denver Glen sent me roses and poetry. I called him and said, 'Drop dead. I ain't going to Denver.' Only at Christmas did I consent to make the trip — to see Brian, not Glen. And again, at least once, I found Glen irresistible. Nevertheless I left. When I called Brian a few days later, he pleaded with me to let him have both his parents. Eleven days later Glen flew to Vancouver with a ring and proposed. I said 'Yes.'

"We called Eba. She sent earrings and this pearl necklace. Then we flew to Hawaii to visit Eba —14 years to the day from our first meeting. Eba, who was sick, told us, 'Now that I've seen you I can go.' Five weeks later she died." A gentleman who had taken my Fantastic First Impression seminar happened to overhear Marsha's amazing narrative. He remembered the suggestion to ask women about their jewelry. With wide eyes he looked at me and exclaimed, "It works!"

Conversation Pieces

You can make it easier for others to ask you a question if you wear something that either stands out, like a loud tie or ornate necklace, or a curiosity piece. I reduced the cover of my book, *Get In Bed With Your Audience And Satisfy Them EVERY Time*, to little larger than a postage stamp, laminated it and used duct tape to attach a safety pin to the back. Now I can wear it on my shirt or lapel. When someone asks what it is, I tell him or her and add: "If I had one on my back, I could audition for a sandwich board."

For minimal investment you can make yourself a similar conversation piece. Use an art card with a favorite painting or sculpture. Hang a small bolt on a chain. When people ask its significance, say, "I attract so many nuts I bought a bolt."

The more unusual or unlikely the object, the better it works. I've gotten the best results with an ornate lizard pin worn on my shoulder. Women, especially, comment on it or ask my reason for wearing such an outlandish accessory. "To tempt you to talk to me," I tell them.

Chapter Two:
Conversation Tips

Communicate With Flair

Three things are paramount in the determination of a person's success in life:

1. Emotional intelligence, or the ability to get along with others.
2. Motivation, or degree of drive.
3. Communication skills, or how effectively ideas and information are articulated.

The three are inter-related. Emotional intelligence embraces communication skills, especially in the area of saying things tactfully. Motivation leads us to improve our emotional intelligence, which, unlike IQ, is subject to betterment. Motivation also prompts us to develop communication skills enabling us to speak and listen in a way that gains the respect of others.

During a first meeting with someone, our emotional intelligence and motivation level are less apparent than our ability to listen and put our ideas into concise, interesting and understandable form. One way to do this is to exhibit a wide repertoire of words. A good place to start an active vocabulary enlargement program is with adjectives. I suggest you eliminate from your everyday usage those adjectives whose overuse has dulled their impact to that of a rusted paring knife beaten repeatedly against a granite wall. The most overused and, hence, flimsy of those adjectives is the ubiquitous "great." Sportscasters are some of the worst offenders. They describe a well-performed play and a superior player as "great." The only other adjective in their anemic arsenal is "outstanding."

When a sportscaster uses "good," it's to describe success. "The Bears have had good success running the ball." Because success is itself good (Have you ever heard of "bad" success?), "good" becomes redundant.

Another word commonly misused is "indicate." It connotes a suggestion rather than statement of fact. During the O.J. Simpson trial, the judge and lawyers used it so often some people might have wondered if it was a legal term. Invariably the word they should have used was "say" or "tell." If on Monday an attorney says, "We will conclude our case tomorrow," this remark on Tuesday should be referenced, "Yesterday you said (not indicated) you'd finish today."

Sportscasters work in a visual medium where words are but adjuncts to the action. When we are one-on-one with a new acquaintance, we don't have that advantage. Nor do we have a captive audience. Therefore our vocabulary becomes both a mark of our verbal ability and a tool for making conversation more enjoyable for persons we speak to. Vary your adjectives and you'll have done a lot to improve your CQ (conversation quotient).

Instead of "great" try some of these words: adept, proficient, excellent, formidable, consummate, incomparable, unparalleled, brilliant, remarkable, or extraordinary. If you catch yourself falling into a habit of using a single—or even a few— adjectives to the exclusion of all others, concentrate on coming up with fresh ones. Which words you use, or even misuse, is less important than having a variety. Variety is the spice of life. Conversation is a part of life, so spice up your conversation. It makes talking more fun.

Where I attended college in Southern California, guys had a catchall word of praise. Whatever they approved of they called "bitchin'." To express a higher degree of approval they said "way bitchin'." Twenty-five years later I made it to a reunion. The new California term of endearment was "intense." It reached its logical limit of absurdity, I thought, when a woman sitting next to me on a rafting trip pointed to one of the many look-alike arroyos lining the river and said, "That looks like a pretty intense little canyon."

Prepare For Whom You'll Meet

If you know whom you'll be meeting, do some homework. Arrive informed. Armed with information about the company you hope to join, you can relate your unique skills to the specific needs of the prospective employer. Likewise, sales persons can show how their product or service will meet existing and future needs of the potential customer.

In social settings, you can prepare by observing the people around you. Who is obviously gregarious? These are the easiest people to meet. Who seems reserved? A quieter, low-key approach works with them better than if you come on like a SWAT squad breaking down a bandit's door. Are some touchy-feely types present? With them you want to hold the handshake a little longer.

Ask questions. "What's the biggest change your business faces?" "Of what is your company most proud?" "What's the most satisfying thing about your job?" "The most challenging?"

It's better to pursue one topic with follow-up questions than to skip around. You want to appear interested in what you asked about rather than just throwing out questions for the sake of conversation. The old "Where are you from? What's your sign? Come here much?" routine is real shallow.

Use Examples

When you respond to a question with a general statement, add an example. It will give credibility to your remark and make it — and you — more memorable. For example, if you say you think athletes are overpaid, site an example of one who makes tons of money and posts mediocre numbers year after year. If you declare the stock market is about to take a downturn, mention the indicators leading you to this prediction.

Watch Your "But"

To express disagreement, start with "and" rather than "but." "But" is a rapport killer; it nullifies what the other person just said. At best, it implies disagreement. "And," on the other hand, connects thoughts without undermining them. Suppose someone tells you, "I believe capital punishment is appropriate for the most heinous crimes." If you reply, "But we sometimes execute innocent people," it has an aggressive tone. You'd do better to say, "No question that some crimes may warrant the extreme penalty, and I'd be more inclined to support it if we weren't at risk of executing an innocent person."

The second response validates the person's reasoning rather than discounting it. "But" is often shorthand for, "You're full of crap." Prefacing the "but" with "yeah" is no protection. If anything, the "yeah" adds to the distastefulness of the "but." Chronic users of the "Yeah, but" turn it into a single word. You need just a few "yeahbut"s to sound obnoxious.

Take Out The Garbage

Eschew no-brainer words and phrases like "you know" and "basically." People who preface their every factual statement with one or the other sound like idiots—probably even to each other. I've heard well-educated adults in management positions run "basically" into the ground. "Basically, we have two divisions. One deals basically with production. The other basically takes care of distribution. That's it, basically." In addition to misusing the word, they compound the folly with over-use.

The insertion of "basically" into a declarative sentence without a modifier is a waste of four syllables. If I say, "Basically, we meet twice a month," the "basically" adds nothing to the sentence's meaning. Suppose I say, "Basically, we meet twice a month but occasionally a third time, if circumstances so warrant." Here the "basically" helps to establish that bi-monthly meetings are the norm.

"Like" is another word to beware of. Some teenagers can't tell you the time of day without it. "Like it's half past four. Is that like later than you thought?" The distinction between "like" and "such as" is a grammatical nuance ignored even by some English professors (in speech, if not writing). The gratuitous use of "like" in even casual speech, much less at first meeting, is best left alone.

The word's defenders claim "like" is an interjection that can serve both as a pause while the speaker gathers the next word and as a way of connoting informality. It says, "We're friends; we can be casual." In the youth culture that has blossomed since World War II, even some adults strive to sound more like younger people. If you want to sound like your kids, say "like" a lot. It's like your choice.

Pitch Your Imperatives

Sometimes in our enthusiasm about something, a film, for example, we're inclined to say, "You really should see it." Of a place we think our partner would appreciate, we might blurt, "You've got to go there." Or if the person has mentioned he or she contemplates a particular project, we might encourage him or her with, "Yes, you must do it."

Despite the well-meaning intent behind this kind of affirmation, it can come off a bit uppity. Expressions such as "should," "have to," "must," "need to," carry a hint of moralizing. They can make you sound preachy, or like a know-it-all. If you think someone would benefit from getting married, enlisting in the military, or going on a diet, you can suggest actions without use of an imperative. Just say, "Have you ever considered...?" or "Maybe you'd find it useful to..." or "What are your thoughts about...?"

Few of us like others to tell us what to do. We especially don't like people we've just met to offer unsolicited advice too emphatically. The ideal way to give advice is to let the person you're talking to think your idea was his or her own. To do this, be roundabout. Make your suggestions off-handedly in a non-moralizing way. For example, "What do you think might happen if...?" That gives your partner a chance to articulate just what you had in mind.

Tell A Terrific Tale

The more open and emotionally accessible you seem, the more comfortable people will feel with you. Making people feel comfortable goes a long way toward a fantastic first impression. To put people more at ease, tell a self-effacing story about yourself. If you show you can laugh at your own vulnerability, people will have more respect for you. They will also relax and reveal more about themselves.

Think of any of the many times you've embarrassed yourself. Work on relating the incident with just enough detail to make it easy to visualize. If other people played roles in the scenario, speak their words in their voices. Exaggerate for effect. Keep the story brief. If possible, have a punch line. Tell the story to friends. Ask what would make it funnier. Hone the anecdote until it has some entertainment value. If you get a laugh—or just a smile—in the process of self-disclosing, you've gone a long way toward creating rapport.

I remember a double date I went on in high school. We were on a country road, headed for a picnic site, in my blue Pontiac convertible, when BOOM—a tire blew out. Neither I nor the other guy knew how to change a tire. So our dates got out of the car and changed it while we watched. In time I overcame the humiliation, but I've never transcended the adverse relationship to things mechanical the incident previewed. To this day, if I get a bike tire patched, it's a moral victory.

This story, told with greater or lesser detail, depending on the situation, has served me for years. When the subject of computers comes up, it's a natural for making fun of my lack of operating facility. Sometimes I add: "I even tried to improve our relationship by naming the machines. The computer is Methuselah because it's so old. The printer is Tortuga (Spanish for turtle) because it's so slow." Having more than one story is even better. Multiple stories give you flexibility; you're more likely to have one suitable for different topics of conversation and less likely to get tired of hearing yourself tell the same tale repeatedly. Any story falling too often from the same lips begins to limp. Add new twists or details to give old time worn tales new legs. You'll be as grateful as your listeners.

Build A Word Bank

My aunt Rachel used to complain of having no friends. This, she said, was why she always looked so sour. When I visited her not long ago, she looked radiant. I asked what accounted for the change.

"Oh Gary, I took a vocabulary class and learned a wonderful new word. Now when anyone tells me some personal good news—like 'My child won a scholarship,' or 'My husband got a promotion'—I say, 'Stupendous!"

"What did you used to say instead of 'stupendous'?"

"Bullshit."

Rachel had discovered the magic of words. Getting the right one in the right place makes a huge difference in the way people perceive us. To get the right one requires having more than a few in our working vocabulary—the words we use on a regular basis.

A better than average vocabulary is likely to make you a better than average communicator and certain to make you more interesting to listen to. Forget the reverse snobbery edict that says using words your listeners aren't used to distances you from them. All but the genetically obtuse and intellectually deprived appreciate word power.

Let Your Body Talk

Words are essential to the communication of thoughts and facts. The thoughts and facts they communicate, however, are not the most important part of a first impression. Energy is. You can actually raise another person's energy by showing lots of it yourself. Unless you come across as a person who gives every indication of severe depression, I recommend you not just match but try to better him or her a bit in enthusiasm. This isn't normally difficult because most people go through the motions of an introduction in no more than middle gear. Just a little more visible excitement on your part will convey your delight at the encounter and make the other person feel you really meant it when you said, "I'm happy to meet you."

No less an authority than my friend Leil Lowndes, author of two excellent books on relating to others, suggests matching the other person's mood. If he or she is laid back, you want to lie back too. Likewise, if you meet someone who is bouncing off walls, you go into manic mode as well. My reason for disdaining what may be sound advice is: we all have ways to disguise our true moods for the sake of social convention. The mood meeting our eye may not be the person's real mood. Furthermore, if we become too focused on discerning a person's mood for the purpose of matching it, we are less attuned to more important parts of the encounter, like what someone is saying. That makes us less present.

The way to convey more energy is to move much more than your mouth when you talk. For example, if you say something thrilled you, bounce on the balls of your feet. If you describe something as tiny, show how tiny by holding your thumb and forefinger barely apart. You can show largeness by spreading both arms or raising a hand above your head. A hand movement from your chest out to your side and around behind you enlivens your statement that something happened "a long time ago." Animation is energy. Energy is contagious. Be generous with your energy and people will all but genuflect.

Kill Your Clichés

I had an English professor named Jack David Angus Ogilvy. He had a Ph.D. from Harvard, was an acclaimed scholar, and held in contempt anyone who degraded the English language by using hackneyed phrases. One mean winter morning, we crossed paths in the quad. The tall, lean professor wore a wool garment that covered his entire head and face except for his eyes. "By Jove," I exclaimed, "You look like the Ghost of Hamlet." He replied, "I intend to keep warm even if I stick out like a sore thumb."

His choice of words surprised me. This bastion of good usage, this pillar on the temple of fresh phrasing had committed a semantic sin. "Stick out like a sore thumb"—only the cold, I thought, could have brought this esteemed academic to utter such a blatant cliché.

If Professor Ogilvy could so slip, anyone can. This means we

need to guard against this egregious offense with all the more
vigor. Instead of sticking out like a sore thumb you can be as
obvious as an aircraft carrier in a swimming pool. Instead of
avoiding something like the plague you can evade it the way you
would lancing a boil. If you like anatomical references to
describe extremes of temperature, eschew the common coinage
and say it was "breezier than a bruja's bosom." Find fresh ways
to express common sentiments and you won't be left feeling like
a one-legged person in a kicking contest, much less a mouse at
an elephant convention.

Forswear Fast Familiarity

Assumption is the mother of misunderstanding. Never
assume a Richard wants to be called Dick, or an Elizabeth finds
Liz pleasing. Use the name people give when they introduce
themselves until further notice. If you can't remember if the gentleman said Robert or Rob, ask. "Do you prefer Robert or Rob?"
That's a sign of respect.

Extroverted people are quicker than introverts to invite you
to call them by the short form of their name. Extroverts also
tend to call others by short forms faster, often without invitation. Six times out of seven it may give no offense. Then there's
always the Penelope who hates Penny because her brother teased
her with "Penny candy, cheap and handy." You call her Penny and
you become identified, if only subconsciously, with her onetime
tormentor.

Names, although common, are very personal. We carry part
of our self-identity in our name or nickname. When others honor
the name we wish to be called by, we are grateful for the courtesy.

Leave Your Sad Baggage At Home

Exponent of self-disclosure that I am, I still balk at laying a lot of personal sorrow on a new acquaintance. Confessing too quickly to struggling with whether or not to leave your spouse, declare bankruptcy, or commit yourself to a mental institution can unnerve a new friend. He or she will wonder if you want sympathy or advice—and probably isn't prepared to provide much of either. Keep things light for a while. Don't put people on the spot by assuming they want to hear on first meeting what troubles your soul. Even after you've gotten to know someone well enough to spill your guts, do so only if you are willing to have his or hers spilled back.

Accept Praise Gracefully

When you receive a compliment (and if you practice the advice of this book you'll get many), add a tagline to your thanks. Suppose, ladies, someone says how good your hair looks. Don't stop with the merely polite "Thank you." Add to it, "How kind of you to comment." You can go even further with something like, "I was a little nervous about this new arrangement. You've just made my day."

Suppose, gentlemen, a new acquaintance comments favorably about your tie. If you picked it out yourself, say how much you appreciate having your taste confirmed by another connoisseur of clothing. If your spouse, daughter, or girlfriend selected it, say she'll be pleased to hear it made a hit.

Abundant gratitude is a powerful tool for making people feel good about themselves. At even a small compliment, show delight above and beyond the call of convention and you'll lend a glow to the giver's spirit. When you help someone else to glow, you become brighter in his or her eyes.

Pin Your Talk On Their Topic

People usually give you clues to what they'd like to talk about. The clues can be subtle. "Snow is like love: You never know when it will arrive or how long it will last." The speaker of this maxim probably wants to talk about skiing or romance. Or the clues can be so blatant as not to be mere clues, but announcements.

I remember a party date with a woman named Monique. She was an avid fan of a college football team whose coach had just announced, to the surprise of the sports world, his retirement. She had barely greeted me when she blurted, "What do you think about Coach McCartney's resignation?" Not as it mattered what I thought; she just wanted me to know what she thought.

On the long drive to the party, Monique spoke of nothing else. She speculated on the reasons for the retirement and vented her disdain for the decision. I listened as patiently as could reasonably be expected by someone indifferent to the situation. Let her vent now, I thought, so we can enjoy the party later.

Little did I know this was but Monique's warm-up. At the party, she engaged anyone who would listen and ran through her array of reasons and condemnations, again and again, with no waning of vigor.

Having heard it all once, I found other people to talk to. My inattentiveness to Monique and her topic left her thinking less of me. Her extended compulsion to express her views on the topic left me thinking less of her. Alas, it was the beginning of yet another end.

Moral of the story: If you meet a Monique and want to impress her or him (Moniques come in both genders), take up the topic she or he hits you with. Moniques have a greater need to talk about their topic than you do not to. If you have neither interest in nor knowledge of it but want to make a good impression anyway, try the next technique. It's a little transparent but damned if it doesn't work.

When All Else Fails...Parrot

Let's face it, some people are harder to talk to than others. If you find yourself laboring to keep a conversation going because you don't know what to ask next, try playing parrot. Whatever the other person says, just repeat the last word or few words with a rising inflection so it sounds like a question.

Suppose the person you're talking to says, "I just got my '73 Chevy Supreme an MKV SuperX." You don't want him (more likely than her) to think you a fool, so you hesitate to ask, "What's an MKV SuperX?" For all you know it could be a motor, ham radio, or convertible top, which is fine. You don't have to ask what it is. Instead, repeat "MKV SuperX" as though it were a question. The gentleman may think you're asking why he chose that model over another. In any case, he'll have more information to impart. "Yeah, it's got four hundred sixty horses and a retractable blow-back."

Now you have another phrase to parrot. "Retractable blow-back?" Your partner can now tell you why this feature is so appealing to him. Whether the beauty of a blowback beguiles you or not is less important than how good you're making the man feel by showing interest in his passion.

Terminate Tactfully

Difficult as you may find it to initiate a conversation, getting out sometimes proves even harder. You don't want to hurt your new acquaintance's feelings by making him or her think you're bored. It would undo the very impression you labored to create. So how do you say good-bye in an upbeat way?

If you're in a social setting with other people present, try something like, "I'm really glad we met. You're fun to talk to, Alice. Maybe we can talk more later or at another time. Right now, there are some other people here I need to connect with. Will you excuse me?" The wording doesn't matter, as long as you 1) express gratitude for the meeting, using his or her name, 2) pay the person a compliment, 3) ask permission to move on. It could take the form, "Ray, the ideas you shared have given me something to think about. It's been a treat talking to you, and I hope we'll get to again. Now let's mingle. OK?"

If you're genuinely pressed for time, say so and ask for the person's phone number so you can call and finish the conversation. If he or she provides it, make the call. It will strongly reinforce a positive first impression. When you call, you may face the same dilemma: How to extricate yourself gracefully. Simply state at the outset that you have only so much time to spare right now but wanted to connect anyway.

I remember a woman with whom I initiated a conversation at a party. Our exchange was brief, perfunctory, and, I thought, unencumbered by romantic undercurrent. The next day she called and said, "Sorry to bother you but I just want to tell you what a captivating face you have." Before I could utter a thank you, she said goodbye and hung up.

A sucker for any kind of compliment, I called her back and suggested we get together— which we did, and did again. By the time I realized the surprise compliment was a standard technique of hers for compelling the interest of males, I was hooked. Though the relationship proved rocky, I learned one valuable lesson. If you want to make a big hit quickly, call your new acquaintance soon after your first meeting and say something real nice.

If you want to make an even bigger hit and are willing to wait, ask the person what he or she would like to be remembered for. The answer will tell you about his or her idealized self-image. Let a little time go by then call with a compliment of the quality or achievement he or she hopes will receive recognition. Now you've put yourself in a warm corner of the person's heart.

Chapter Three:
Bringing Others Together

Put A Hook On Introductions

Every time you have a chance to introduce two people, say more than "Ralph, this is Tom. Tom, this is Ralph." Make it easier for Ralph and Tom to talk to each other. Give any tidbit you can to each. "Tom, Ralph collects wine bottle corks. Ralph, Tom trains guide dogs."

If you've just met one of them and know nothing about the other, at least tell the newcomer to the conversation anything you can about the one you've already talked to a few minutes. Or you can fill the newcomer to the group in on what you're talking about. "Ralph, Tom and I were just discussing whether there are limits to forgiveness in personal relationships, and if so, what they are. We hope you'll join our little colloquy."

Maybe all you can say about someone is what his or her profession is. That's OK, just spruce up the job description. "Leah, Christine takes really fabulous photos of everything from buildings to bar mitzvahs." Christine feels good about the compliment, and Leah finds it easier to say something to Christine, even if it's only, "What's your favorite thing to photograph?"

When you play host in this way, you're active. People admire both your energy and your eagerness to bring others together. In her book *How To Work A Room*, Susan Roane says successful socializers combine charm and chutzpah. Charm is about being pleasant, funny, and smiling. Chutzpah means having nerve, even intrepidness. Take initiative in a warm way to make it easier for other people to meet each other. This will gain you their esteem in a hurry by showing you value yourself and others.

Create A "Crowd"

When you see two people talking and want to join them, approach them and wait till whoever is speaking finishes a thought. There's always a chance one of the participants will acknowledge your presence and invite you to join them. If not, say, "You look as though you're having a very interesting conversation. If it's not a private matter you're discussing, would you mind if I join you?"

The very fact that you took this initiative should give you stature in their eyes. If you find yourself talking to one person and another person walks up, jump at the chance to invite him or her into the conversation. The old saying, "Two 's company, three 's a crowd" applies only if the two have a romantic agenda. In a social setting, two 's company, and three is more company. Go for it!

Of course, if you perceive that they are indeed having a private conversation, look for a three or foursome to attach yourself to. If a man and woman look as though they're in the initial stage of relationship we'll call, for lack of a better word, flirting, respect their probable preference for privacy and pass by. The same goes for two people of either gender who look as though they're negotiating a deal. The larger the group, the easier time you'll have joining it anyway. You have a better chance of getting someone's attention, and privacy obviously isn't an issue.

Now what do you do if you're one of the two people having a private business or romance conversation and a third party tries to intrude? Be courteous. Smile and ask the person's name. Introduce yourself and the party you're talking to. Thank the third person for wishing to join you, then explain that you're handling some important business and ask if you can talk to him or her later. If the person waxes apologetic, say, "No need to apologize. You couldn't have known. Thanks for understanding." Then make sure to seek the person out later, even if only to repeat your appreciation.

Chapter Four:

Answering The Predictable Questions

Where You're From

Whether you grew up in one place and moved to another or just stayed put, you can give a more interesting answer to the inevitable "Where are you from?" if you embellish it. Instead of saying no more than Dallas, DesMoines, Detroit, or DePaul, provide a little local color. You could say something like, "I was born in Eureka Springs, AR, home of the world famous Frog Museum. When I was five, my family moved to Joplin, MO, where Mickey Mantle first played professional baseball."

This tactic gives your partner an opportunity to ask another, related question. "How many frogs are in the frog museum?" Or, "Did you ever see Mantle play?" At any first meeting, you want to make it easy for your new acquaintance to ask questions and keep the conversation moving along.

Suppose you're from the very place most of your new encounters occur. You can offer a bit of not widely known information about the place. "I'm from right here in Palooka Ville, founded in 1849 by two gold miners who flipped a raccoon to decide after which of them to name their stake." Or you can drop a startling biographical fact. "I was born here, in a hospital six blocks from where I now live in a house less than a block from the one I grew up in." (For me, this is true.)

What You Do

Probably the most frequently asked question after "Where are you from?" is "What do you do?" At least it's the case in American culture. (The French consider it rude to inquire of a stranger what his or her vocation is—too personal.) Most people respond to the vocation question with a simple label: Teacher, lawyer, butcher, baker, or candlestick maker. There's nothing terribly wrong with this kind of answer. There's not much right about it either, except for its surface accuracy.

We use labels for their convenience; they save us time. They also promote stereotyping that creates barriers to understanding, interest, and rapport.

When someone asks what you do, he or she is not just seeking information. The person is trying to keep up a conversation. If your answer provides inadequate information or fails to keep the conversation moving along, you might want to revise it.

The most common stereotype for an artist is of a nonconformist who scrapes by with the help of a part-time job. For a plumber, we think of someone with his sleeves rolled up and muck on his arms, one who never arrives on time and still charges lots of money, which we gladly pay rather than get muck on our arms. We think of estate planners as bland folks who write wills according to legal requirements.

To overcome these and other stereotypes, I suggest you have a way of describing your work that goes beyond the labels. Develop a brief description of your activity and the way people benefit from it. For example, an artist might say, "I use pigment to produce images that bring more color into people's work and living space." A plumber could say, " I keep pipes clean so that people can live in cities under sanitary conditions." An estate planner might say, "I create documents to ensure your belongings end up where you want them to when you're no longer here."

This kind of response to the question of vocation both shows you to be a person of imagination and gives the person talking to you an easy opening for more questions. Having the other person ask another question is just what you want. The idea is not to give your job title, much less a complete description of your duties, but to keep the conversation moving along. It also answers the question, which was "What do you do?" not "What is your job title?"

If the person you're talking to asks any question at all — "How do you do that?" or "For whom do you do that?" or "Are you a _____?" – you succeeded. Now you can give more information about your job, the activity it entails and the way this activity benefits others.

Suppose someone tells you he or she is an astro-geophysicist. If you don't know what that is, you can ask and risk looking uninformed, or think of another question. If you have to think of another question, an awkward pause occurs. It would have been easier for you if the astro-geophysicist had said, "I test rockets so that they land where they're supposed to, which saves you tax dollars."

Including the actual or potential benefit to others, especially the person in front of you, is important. It makes your answer "existential," or relevant to real life people. I know a photographer who, after taking one of my classes, stopped saying, "I'm a photographer." Now she says, "I stop time to preserve your image." This response, she told me, not only makes meeting people more fun, it has gotten her more business.

I could say of my job, "I work with individuals and organizations to help them get the most out of their spoken words, with the result that they communicate with power and passion."

In a business setting, you can make your answer into a brief commercial. A useful formula for constructing such a "twenty second zinger" is simple:

1. State a common problem you can alleviate.
2. Tell an important benefit of your product or service.
3. Say how people feel when they get the benefit.

Here's how I might do this: "Have you ever wondered if your presentations are as clear, concise, and convincing as they could be? I can show you how to increase your personal charisma, so that your audiences feel better about you, and you feel better about yourself."

This way of telling people what you do doesn't work for everyone. A woman in one of my seminars said, "I don't want to waste time with what begins to sound like a guessing game. Just tell me your job title, and I'll know what you do. If I'm in doubt, I can ask." I respect her point of view without sharing it.

In the same seminar, we had a psychiatrist. He pointed out that knowing he was a psychiatrist didn't tell much about what he did. He could evaluate people accused of crimes for the purpose of determining their mental competency to stand trial. Or he might test children for learning disabilities and recommend special educational measures. A psychiatrist could also care for people confined to a mental institution, counsel couples experiencing marital difficulties, or conduct research on the effectiveness of particular drugs for different symptoms.

Our psychiatrist thought for a few minutes about how he could tell people what he did and decided on: "I let people tell me what's not working in their lives and then help them achieve a higher level of freedom to make meaningful choices." In the same seminar, the director of a chamber of commerce for a large shopping center came up with: "I show store owners ways to maximize their profits so that you have more shopping options."

This way of describing your job humanizes what might otherwise sound abstract, vague, or even threatening. Consider a police officer in one of my classes. He came up with: "I respond to domestic disputes to minimize the risk of violence." He could just as well have said: "I enforce traffic laws to make it safer for you to drive in the city." Either beats "I'm a cop."

Important to notice is that the officer didn't include all his duties. One suffices, especially if it's easy to visualize. The more concrete and specific your description, the better. Avoid abstract words like "computer," "design," and even "teach." I think, "Show how to" is more graphic than "teach." You'd think it pretty cool if an accountant, for whom the common stereotype is someone fonder of numbers than people, said, "I show you how to keep as much of your money as is legally possible in your pocket instead of the Fed's."

Instead of asking, "What do you do?" you might try "What's your area of expertise?" This not only shows you assume they have special skill or knowledge; it also protects the feelings of people temporarily out of work or retired. A person recently laid off or fired may be embarrassed to tell you. He or she still has an area of expertise and can speak of it proudly.

Another way to frame the question is, "What's your main activity?" This gives the person the option of telling you about a vocation or another way he or she spends time. If the response is, "Looking for work," ask what kind of work he or she seeks.

My personal approach is never to ask someone what he or she does until the person asks me. I prefer to ask questions less designed to help me classify someone and aimed more at getting to know what his or her interests, even passions, are.

We like it when people demonstrate they are aware that we're more than our resumes, job descriptions, and other such non-vital statistics.

Chapter Five:

Conversation Currency

Talk Takes Topics

To have even a rudimentary conversation we need subjects. Often the situation in which you meet someone dictates an initial topic. If you meet in a ticket line to a theatrical production, you can ask, "What have you heard about the play?" If you meet during an intermission, "What do you like best about the play so far?" If on the way out, "How does the play compare to others you've seen?"

Notice that all of these questions invite more than "yes" or "no" answers. Even "How did you like the play?" may get a single word response, like "fine." Give your new friend a chance to say more, rather than less, about his or her thoughts. "What did you think?" is a weak question. Even though it may draw a lengthy response, its vagueness may leave the person wondering how to respond. When someone asks me, as people often do, what I "thought" of an art exhibition, I never know what detail they want me to go into. So I say "very interesting," or "quite impressive," or just "OK."

When a waiter asks, "How's everything?" I tend to be more specific. "The salad is limp, the corn undercooked, and the smoothie insipid." That or an equally positive assessment of each item gets a look of surprise. Try it.

The more topics you can comfortably converse about, the smoother your social path. We admire people who know a whole lot about one thing. The philosopher Isaiah Berlin called them hedgehogs because they burrow so deep into their subject. Yet unless we are interested in their area of expertise, we find it easier to converse with people who know a little about a lot of things, called foxes by Berlin. The more things of general interest you have in your conversational repertoire, the better your chance of making a good first impression. You need know only a little about something to make a few intelligent observations and, better, ask intelligent questions. No need to be like the big name recording star who, when told that his CD topped the chart in Austria, said, "Where's that?"

Let's talk about some topics you can always talk about with most anyone.

News Of The Day

In college I worked as an announcer at a local television station. The hardest part of the job was the morning interview program. I didn't know who the guests were until I arrived at the station shortly before we went on. One fateful day, a pilot and flight attendant showed up. Their airline had just ended a long strike, and these company representatives were in the studio to advertise this fact. Although both had flown for many years, they proved resistant to interrogation. Whatever I thought to ask, they gave, at best, single sentence answers.

"Are you pleased to be working again?"

"Yes."

What did you miss most about flying?"

"Oh, I don't know."

"Surely you've had some interesting experiences in your years in the air."

"Mmmm yeah."

"Can you tell our viewers about one?"

"Uh...I can't think of one right now."(Neither of them could!)

With three minutes still left in the program, I had run out of ideas. In desperation I alluded to the spate of plane crashes in the past six months. "When you read about a crash does it make you nervous?" No sooner was the word "crash" out of my mouth than I knew I had done just that. Crashed. Although my guests were nonplussed—one of them shrugged and mumbled, "Not especially"—an officer of the airline took umbrage. He called the station manager, who promptly fired me.

Whether my miscue warranted termination, I leave you to judge. The experience left me resolved never to be as stuck for an answer as my yep and nope interviewees. Conversation is the primary arena in which first impressions occur. To make the best possible impression, be prepared to talk about something of interest to your partner. If your partner tips you off by mentioning his or her love of ontogeny, ontology, or entomology, run with it. Ask questions. Say, "That's fascinating. Please tell me more. How did you first become interested in this area of inquiry?"

If you don't get clues to the person's passion, a good fallback ploy is news of the day, preferably something more momentous than the weather. As I type these words, the United States Congress has just impeached President Clinton. This kind of news will get most anyone's two cents worth. Even on a day when no president was impeached, no bombs dropped on Iraq, no single season seventieth home run hit, and no octuplets born, you can find a piece of news to use as a conversation stimulant. "What would you name the zoo's newborn hippo?" "How, if at all, does the Dow's dive affect your life?" "Do you think there will ever be peace in the Middle East?

Movies

Most people see films, if not often, at least once in a while. To use a movie as conversation currency, simply ask your new friend if he or she has seen any movie lately. That kind of phrasing gives the person an easy out if he or she can't bring one to mind. If you begin by asking about a specific film, and the person hasn't seen it, you have to start over. Make it as easy as possible for him or her to respond in the affirmative. Once the name of a film is mentioned, you can ask what the person found compelling or disappointing about it. As we discuss in the chapter on "Moving from 'Small Talk' to Deeper Things, this is a good way to go from small to large talk, from the customary comfort creators, like "Where are you from?" and "What do you do?" to matters that yield real insight and knowledge about people's deep beliefs and personal passions.

Religion & Politics

We've all heard we should avoid talking about religion or politics. This stricture is nonsense. Respectful, rational adults can talk about any damn thing they like and not offend each other. If you happen to get into a conversation with one of those semi-psychotic people who go through life just looking to be offended, you'll give him or her reason to find fault by whatever you say.

Religion may be a compartment of life, isolated from other compartments except in matters of morals. Politics, on the other hand pervades our lives. We can't escape it. Even talk about sports can include politics, especially if the owners of professional basketball teams and the players association are at such odds that an entire season is threatened. If any professional athlete gets traded for what some see as an attitude problem, that gets into politics, if only those of the locker room.

Religious views surely affect one's view of whether a president deserves impeachment or removal from office for telling lies about extra-marital sex. Whether one thinks a company's foremost responsibility is to its customers, employees, or stockholders may well depend on a system informed by spiritual orientation. Therefore, I find the idea that we should avoid discussion of religion or politics absurd. The only way around those subjects is silence.

Chapter Six:

Communication Styles

Everyone Has A Style

For most of my adult life I thought anyone who had a problem communicating with me must be stupid. After all, I'm direct, candid, and reasonably articulate. If there was a failure to communicate, the onus lay on the other guy.

What I didn't know is that people use language differently. That's what style is: the way we say things. Our personality has a lot to do with our style, as does our sense of what we use language for. Conversation has different meanings and intents for different people, as we'll see in a moment. Yet most of us expect other people to use language the same way we do. When they don't, there's conflict. We talk right past each other then wonder how two intelligent human beings, speaking the same language, could fail so miserably to communicate.

Differences in style need not lead inevitably to communication breakdown. Regardless of our style, if we recognize the other person's and make accommodations to it, the day is saved. We recognize other people's styles by listening carefully. Our unselfconscious conversation is full of clues to our style. Common sense suffices to tell us what adaptations to make in our style to create more rapport with people of another style. And rapport is to communication what light is to vision.

Bottom Liners

Sergeant Joe Friday, played by Jack Webb on the old radio program "Dragnet," was the archetypal bottom liner. When he interviewed a witness and the person began to speculate or emote, Friday interrupted with a terse, "Just the facts."

Bottom liners use language to convey information and negotiate deals. They rarely waste words and don't want other people to either. Wasted words are wasted time. Verbal flourishes in theater or literature are fine; that's the place for them. Include them in ordinary conversation, and the bottom liner tunes you out.

The best way to spot bottom liners is by the brevity of their responses. They favor one word or, at most, single sentence answers. While they may not see alternatives as black and white, they tend to speak as if they did. It's easier for them to categorize a person or situation unfairly than to articulate factors that might mitigate their opinion. Their favorite conversations are short, not necessarily sweet. To those who do not share their style, bottom liners can seem abrasive, even rude.

Detail Freaks

Some people use language to explore ideas fully, to revel in their grasp of all the implications, ramifications and possible consequences of a proposal. Or they want to show how thorough a knowledge they have of a subject. The most exemplary bottom liner was Socrates, as Plato portrays him. Socrates loved nothing more than discourse, especially his own. His method was to ask someone a question, such as "What's justice?" then refute the answer and propose one of his own, always at great length.

The dialogue Socrates engaged others in had a terminal value for him. The quest for answers was far more important than the answers themselves, if there even were such things. By gaining a better understanding of ideas, Socrates thought we moved closer to truth, even if we couldn't quite arrive at it. And the discourse (sometimes called "dialectic") by which we approached truth was itself a fulfilling activity.

Suppose a bottom liner's refrigerator malfunctions and he or she calls a repairman, who happens to be a detail freak. The repairman pulls the panel off the refrigerator, looks at the motor, and says: "Well no wonder you have a problem. Have a look at this. The whozit is worn out, which means the whachamajiggy isn't getting enough juice to fire the whadayacallit, so the something-or-other can't contact the..."

At this point, the impatient bottom liner interrupts. "I don't need to know all that. Just tell me three things: Can you fix it? How long will it take? What will it cost?"

The detail freak repairman now looks sad. He was on a roll, just hitting his stride with, to him, relevant information. "How can this barbarian refrigerator owner not take an interest in the subtle workings of his own machine?" he thinks. Meanwhile, the bottom liner owner wonders if he can trust anyone who talks that much to fix anything, much less a refrigerator.

I remember a breakfast meeting at which the gentleman next to me was left out of the conversation around him. He wore a cast on his arm, which gave me an easy question to bring him in: "How did you hurt yourself?"

Had the man been an orthodox bottom liner, he would have answered, "I broke my arm." A liberal bottom liner might have replied, "I fell off my bike and broke my arm."

The gentleman was, however, a detail freak. He jumped at the opening. "I was riding my bike down in the warehouse district, where there are lots of railroad tracks. Usually I take them straight on and have no problem, but this time I must have approached a rail at the wrong angle. My bike flipped over to the left, which means I must have reached across my body with my right arm, the one that got hurt, to break my fall. Isn't that odd that it wasn't my left arm that took the force? Well, no sooner did I hit the pavement than people started streaming out of warehouses to see if I was OK. That wouldn't happen downtown; people there don't care what happens to anybody else. People who work in the warehouses are much nicer. Boy, am I lucky that's where I had the accident."

At this point he took a breath, and I grasped the opportunity to say, "That's a good story. Thanks for sharing."

"Wait," he said. "I want to tell you what the doctor said."

Telling you what the doctor said—and the complete medical history that led to the diagnosis—is a typical detail freak response to any health related question.

Detail freaks combine knowledge and gregariousness. If you share their interests, they can fascinate you. It's only when such a person is full of him or herself that the verbosity is unbearable.

Massager

Finally we have people who use language to bond. They don't care about facts or ideas as much as they do good vibrations. We converse to become better friends. Once we are good friends, we keep talking to nurture the friendship. Language exists to lubricate relationships.

I once invited a massager friend of mine who was coming to Denver with his wife, to stay at my house. After checking with his wife (more typical of a massager than bottom liner or detail freak), my friend reported, "Thank you so much for your generous offer of hospitality, but Claire indicated a strong preference for us to stay at a hotel." That's massager language. Soften the announcement as much as possible. Use a circuitous phrase like "indicates a strong preference" instead of the blunter "wants." Otherwise, it might sound like just what it is: a refusal.

A massager would rather tell you an untruth—or nothing at all—than something he or she thinks you don't want to hear. They hate to deliver negative data.   Bill Clinton, according to an article in The New Yorker (October 26, 1998), is just such a person. "Clinton always sounds like he is trying to please everyone because he is always trying to please everyone... And since he can't always please everyone he often finds himself obliged to warm the truth a little. This is not because he wishes to deceive you; it's because he wants you to know his heart is in the right place. He cannot bear to be the bringer of bad news."

We can only wonder whether the writer got right Clinton's motive for warming the truth. Self-interest could also be part of the picture. He does provide us with a good description of the massager mindset: Speak no word that could possibly piss off the person you're talking to.

Ask a massager if he or she wants to go to dinner, and you'll hear something like, "Gee, I don't know. Do you want to go to dinner?" If then you ask, "Are you hungry?" you'll probably hear, "Oh I don't know. Do you feel hungry?" If you then switch your tact and say, "Hungry? I'm starved. Let's get a pizza," the massager will cooperate and say, "That sounds like a good idea."

Until you reveal your preference, the massagers won't reveal theirs. They don't want any conflict. Once you make your wishes known, massagers go along. They would rather eat pizza, which they wouldn't want even if they were hungry, than risk a dent in the friendship.

A brilliant literary example of agreement at all cost occurs in *Hamlet*. A courtier named Osric, hat in hand, delivers a message to Hamlet. Massagers are well suited for the job of courtier. They would rather look like fools than contradict their superiors.

Osric: Sweet lord, if your lordship were at leisure, I should impart a thing to you from his Majesty.

Hamlet: I will receive it, sire, with all diligence of spirit.
         Put your bonnet to his right use, 'tis for the head.

Osric: I thank your lordship, it is very hot.

Hamlet: No, believe me, 'tis very cold; the wind is northerly.

Osric: It is indifferent cold, my lord, indeed.

Hamlet: But yet methinks it is very sultry and hot for my complexion.

Osric: Exceedingly, my lord; it is very sultry, as 'twere –
         I cannot tell how.

Not all massagers are as fawning as Osric. Most are gentle souls who love harmony and subordinate their real opinions in order to have it. They avoid controversy because they can't deal with it. For this reason, they often appear indecisive, evasive, or even devious.

Adapting To Another Person's Style

It is easy to recognize another person's style. Adapting your own to accommodate another's style is the challenge. Even people who combine styles usually exhibit only one of them in one-on-one conversation with a new acquaintance. That's the style you want to show deference to.

How To Impress A Bottom Liner: Get To The Point

When talking to a bottom liner, be candid and succinct. Bottom liners value honesty, even if it comes with a sharp edge. Respect the bottom liner's need for the conversation to have an outcome, something that justifies the time invested. The outcome need be no more than meeting and learning a little about you. But the kind of chitchat that puts a massager at ease annoys a bottom liner. He or she is what I call a teleological talker: Conversation requires direction. It should move toward a goal—and quickly. Once the goal is achieved, it's time to move on to another.

If you're a massager, don't take offense at the bottom liner's abruptness. If you're a detail freak, don't be surprised—or dismayed—at signs of impatience from a bottom liner. Just try to conduct the conversation in a straightforward, concise fashion. Remember: two bottom liners can communicate with each other far more effectively than two detail freaks or even two massagers. The two detail freaks will both want to talk at the same time. The two massagers may never find out what each other really thinks.

Managing A Detail Freak: Let Patience Be Your Guide

A detail freak affords you the best opportunity to practice active listening. As he or she rambles on, filling the air with "therefore"'s, "whereas"'s, and "on the other hand"'s, you get to nod, smile, and occasionally exclaim. When the speaker pauses, you can praise his or her comprehension of the problem, knowledge of the subject, or generosity in taking the time to fill you in with such thoroughness. Detail freaks adore flattery.

If you want to contribute to the conversation, say something like, "If you've finished your thought I have something to add. Would you like to hear it?" Detail freaks love it when you ask permission to talk. It helps them to feel in control even when they're not talking.

When a detail freak starts repeating him or herself, ask, "And then what happened?" or "I understand your point. Where do you think that leaves us?" Refrain from saying anything that could be interpreted as, "Will you ever shut up?"

Stroking A Massager: Connection Before Content

Because massagers crave harmony, they value small talk. Conversing about the weather is less likely to produce controversy than whether the President should be impeached. For the same reason, ask only open-ended questions. "How do you feel about your experience in this organization?" is better than, "Do you like working here?" "What do you think might improve the situation?" is better than "Do you plan to make a change?"

To get a candid answer from a massager you have to draw the person out. Once you get him or her talking, say nothing that suggests disagreement. And never interrupt. Contradiction and interruption are sure-fire ways to cause a massager to clam up.

Massagers need to like and be liked before they feel comfortable talking to a stranger. Do everything you can to put them at ease. Speak softly, stay calm, and stand a little to the side of the person instead of facing him or her directly. I learned the stand to the side of a person trick from, of all people, Denver's Director of Animal Control. He told me, during one of our adversarial conversations, that he instructs all his dogcatchers to do that when talking to irate pet owners they've just ticketed. And even though I was aware that he was using the technique on me, I felt less threatened by having him more beside than in front of me.

Chapter Seven:
A Sure Sign Of Sincerity

Listening

The most important communication skill you can have is the ability to listen, and listen well. Some say it's why we have two ears and only one mouth. Nothing does more to make another person feel important than giving him or her your complete, undivided, and intense attention. We are born with the ability to hear. We have to learn to listen.

There are levels of listening. The lowest is mere awareness that someone else is talking without knowing what he or she is saying. Our eyes may be on the speaker but our mind inhabits another realm.

Less superficial, yet only a little more attentive, is when you know what's being said but have your mind on what you'll say when your turn comes. Waiting to talk is not listening, just a shabby replica of it. So is pretending to listen. If you say the things that suggest you're listening—"Yes," "How interesting," "Oh really," etc.—while glancing around the room or reaching for something in your pocket, it's a charade.

A higher level is to pay attention and take in what the other person says but fail to convey that you are doing so. Such impassive listening may be acute; it just doesn't come off in the most positive possible manner. The best impression requires active listening.

Active listening means you keep your eyes on the speaker's. Nod, smile, and show that you're interested. Occasionally bounce back what you just heard: "So you find that...." Ask questions: "How did that make you feel?" "Then what happened?" Active listening is not just hearing what is said. It's also demonstrating that you've heard it, find it interesting, and care.

Good listeners also stay still. If you keep shifting your weight from foot to foot, rubbing your neck, or fiddling with something in your pocket, you'll appear distracted and undermine your sincerity. For those of us who have a hard time standing still, this presents a big challenge.

My cousin Jeff is a nervous, fidgety fellow. I can still see him shuffling his feet and moving his arms back and forth at his wedding—while he was speaking his vows. When he talks on the phone he paces the floor and throws his head from side to side. His favorite activity is watching sports, but he can't just sit and watch. He reads sports pages during time outs, shells and eats peanuts during the action, and, on his team's worst plays, slaps the knee of the person sitting beside him. To ask him to keep still while listening would be like asking Donald Duck to speak Oxford English. But unless you're a compulsive kinetic like Jeff, I recommend keeping still when you listen. Any body movement not in direct response to something said might make you appear less than sincere.

In a class I took called "A Thousand and One Ways To Be Romantic," the teacher told us that the most loving thing you can do for someone is to give him or her your complete attention for an extended period. Nothing conveys care more emphatically than to make someone else feel you have nothing in the world more important to do, at that moment, than hear what he or she has to say. When you listen so as to make others feel good about themselves, you, the listener, bask in reflected glory.

Chapter Eight:
Moving From "Small Talk" To Deeper Things

The Gradual Way

In a way, no talk is "small talk." Even the most banal conversation can serve to bond its participants by giving them an
opportunity to be present for each other. As we saw in the chapter on Greetings, the courtesy words, like "How do you do?" and
"Pleased to meet you," are part of first impressions. Although
the words are mere social conventions without much meaning,
the way we say them is an expression of our personalities and
measure of our presence.

Once the formalities are complete, you may want to know
more about a person—what his or her fears, aspirations, and passions are. Were you to say, "Tell me your greatest fear," you'd
appear rude, even if you had a genuine interest. Even more
obnoxious is: "Tell me all about yourself."

The idea is to move smoothly from social ritual to matters of
the heart. A good way is to ask an unthreatening question.
"What's the best movie you've seen this year?" "What's the most
interesting book or article you've read lately?" Suppose the person tells you the name of a movie or title of a book. Follow up
with a question about the movie or book. "What about it did you
like best?"

Whatever the person says, use the answer as a basis for the
next question. For example, if he or she mentions a character,

ask what about the character was interesting. Then you can ask if the person identifies with the character, and why. The answer will reveal something important about the person's situation. You can also ask how the character in the book or movie dealt with his or her predicament. Then: "What do you think you'd do in similar circumstances? Why?"

Notice that the questions are open-ended. They call for more than "yes" or "no" responses. The questions also stay on the same subject. When someone keeps shifting the topic, we perceive it as a mark of insincerity. A rapid-fire series of questions like, "What's your sun sign?", "Come here much?", "Who does your hair?", comes across as questions simply for the sake of talk rather than any real interest in us.

If your partner mentions having taken a trip, don't ask the usual "How'd it go?", or "Did you have fun?" Those are questions that get you a simple "Fine," or "Yes." Try something like, "What were the most exciting ten minutes of the trip?" or "What's the fondest memory you have of it?" This kind of question elicits a more thoughtful and revealing response. And whatever the answer, it will suggest another good question.

On a ski lift I asked an obviously gregarious woman, "What do you think is the most important thing in life?" Her answer included a description of a party she and her husband had for people who didn't already know each other. They asked the guests to abide by one rule: No one could tell anyone else what he or she did; this kept people from stereotyping others on the basis of their work. Lo and behold, the woman told me, the president of her husband's company and the milkman hit it off big-time and made plans to go hunting together. Had they been aware of the disparity in their social status, they might have doubted they had much in common and not explored their similar interests. It was a revelation, she said, of just how limiting stereotypes based on vocation are.

Getting Quickly To The Core

If you want to jump-start a more meaningful conversation, begin with an unexpected question. Instead of "How are you?", or "What do you do?", try something like, "What's your excuse for being here?" Sometimes I like to say, "Hello. What are the best three things that have happened to you today?" even before shaking hands and exchanging names. After a little discourse about the importance of one of the things the person mentions, you can always say, "My name is _____." The name exchange seems to have a little more energy if some conversation preceded it.

By having talked about something of importance, you and the person have already formed a relationship. Now it's more likely when you get around to names and vocations, you'll take a real interest. After exchanging names, get right back to the important subject. For example, the person might say, "The best thing that happened to me today is my son put his toys away without being asked." Jump on this opening to ask more about the son—his name, what efforts went into getting him to put things away, and his aptitudes. The very fact that people mention their children means they like to talk about them. Make it easy to do just that.

If the person refers to something work related, follow up with a question about the situation or event. "How did you feel?" Was that the first time it happened?" You can also use the statement as the basis for a compliment. For example,

"You must be very conscientious about your work," "I'll bet your company is glad to have you working for them," or "I wish we had someone like you where I work."

Chapter Nine:
Literary Accessories

Nametags

At more and more events we see nametags. For business networking parties, three-day seminars, and professional meetings they have become de rigueur. The advantage to all attendees wearing their names on their chests is that you can start a conversation with strangers and call them by name. The downside is that you have less incentive to remember people's names because you can just reread them.

To make the best use of a nametag, wear it on your right side. You turn your right side toward people to shake hands, so the tag is easier to see. If you write your own name on a blank tag, print it large and legible. A feebly scrawled signature with a thin or dying pen is worse than no tag at all. People will strain to decipher it and think less of you for not having made it easy for them. Think about adding something below your name. Depending on the nature of the gathering, you might put your company, hobby, or favorite food. Now you've given people you meet something to pick up on and ask about.

If you want to have some fun at an informal gathering, write no more than Name Tag. Have some witty rejoinders for the remarks you'll encounter. When someone asks if you were named for an ancestor, say, "No, for a horse. But my mother was dyslexic, so instead of Tame Nag I got this."

Business Cards

The purpose of the business card is to provide an attractive, easy to store record of your name and how to reach you for persons who in fact want to reach you. I find it presumptuous to thrust your card into the face—or just hand—of everyone you meet, and wasteful to ask for someone else's card if you have no intention of using it. To request a card for no other reason than to add a name to your company's bulk mailing list smacks of privacy invasion. My inclination, when asked for my card by someone who seems to be acting on the basis of convention rather than conviction, is to ask, "What do you want it for?" The one sure reaction this produces is surprise. And automatic card requesters are at a loss. This isn't the best first impression technique, but it does save you cards.

Have you ever seen a business card with print so fine you need a magnifying glass to make it out? Of course you have; we all have. Some of the things we want to say to the person whose card it is: " Fire your graphic designer." "Is your printer trying to save ink?" " Does this come with a magnifying glass?"

The most egregious case of tiny type I ever saw was on the card of a self-styled art consultant, a name-dropping Easterner who had come to Denver to teach taste to the culturally deprived provincials she thought all westerners were. She even affected an alternative pronunciation of her common last name. Now every time someone gives me an overly designed card I can barely read, I associate the bearer with the Pathetic Pretender.

The current rage is to put your photo on your card. Yes, this makes it easier for people to remember you. Ask yourself, however, if people need help remembering you, is there much point in giving them a card to begin with? Ask yourself also if you would be more intrigued by an eye-catching logo or illustration than someone's face? Finally ask, what message you send when you present a new acquaintance with a photo of yourself? Might not a caricature of you doing whatever it is you do be more suitable? The exception would be if your face were vital to your business.

For my own card I reproduced a painting I did of Long's Peak, one of Colorado's best known mountains. People enjoy the image and often ask questions about it. That's good. We want questions; they aid conversation. The card is larger than standard, which means it can't go easily into a card pile. That could cut either way. People may be more likely to discard it because it won't fit where it's supposed to, or they may keep it somewhere visible, like on the frig. At least the oversize format lets me give more information without crowding the typography.

When you're at an event where business cards get passed out like hard candy on Halloween, take a moment to note on those you collect something about the person and the date. It will help you remember what card goes with what person later. Unless you're gathering names and addresses to sell to a junk mailer, it serves little purpose to have a drawer full of cards from people you can't remember having met.

Your card is an extension of yourself, albeit a small one. Make it reflective of how you want people to think of you—classy, quirky, artistic, iconoclastic, direct, formal, even outrageous. I know a tax consultant who lists his appellate court victories against the Internal Revenue Service on a folding card. If your company has a standard card for all its employees, you can still have a personal card for non-business contacts—it's your First Amendment privilege.

Brochures

That constitutional privilege extends to brochures as well. Better, however, not to exercise it unless there's a clear and present call to do so. In all but sales oriented meetings, first impressions suffer when you instantly try to turn someone you've just met into a customer. Some go-getters will act as though a birthday party is a chamber of commerce networking session. They rarely come away with new clients—or get invited to the host's next party.

Once you've built some rapport, you can offer to show a new acquaintance your brochure or other advertising material. Give the person the option of returning or keeping it. When you thrust it into his or her hand with, "Here, take this," you've probably just wasted your paper and robbed your rapport. A smoother move would be to say something like, "If you're seriously considering using a service like ours in the near future, let me know and I'll send you a brochure." This doesn't put the person on the spot and gives you an opportunity to demonstrate your sincerity by following through later.

A consultant friend of mine thinks it better to give the brochure at first meeting, so the recipient doesn't have to wait to get the information. I don't think my friend appreciates how high a percentage of unsolicited brochures get trashed, if not instantly, surely eventually.

Chapter Ten:
What To Eschew: Tried & True Turnoffs

Risky Wit

Some of us love jokes—all kinds of jokes. Some people like some kinds of jokes. Other people don't like jokes at all. Those, my friends, are insufficient odds to lead off with what you think is a funny story. We live in an age of victim mentality. Lots of "groups" perceive humor based on racial, ethnic, or gender stereotypes as demeaning and, therefore, offensive. While most lawyers relish lawyer jokes, people of Polish descent seldom praise Polish jokes. So be careful with your humor. First meetings make an uncertain forum for airing any but the most innocent attempts at levity.

If wit is so essential to your style that you are about to burst with your newest story, run a tolerance test first. Ask the people you've just met if they've heard any good jokes lately? If their eyes light up with anticipation—either of telling or hearing one—you've got your first clue. If a person then asks how many anybodies it takes to replace a light bulb, you've got your second and sufficient indicator.

What if the response is, "No, have you?" That's probably grounds to proceed—but gently. Don't lead off with the grossest joke you know. If the person to whom you speak is of the opposite sex, refrain for a while from reciting pieces that contain worrisome words, those you can't say on television or read in family newspapers.

The safest ploy is to let humor arise from the situation. If someone commends you on your firm grip, say, "As one suitcase said to the other, 'You're a good grip yourself.'" Witticisms that appear spontaneous even if not, make you look witty. Canned jokes may make you look contrived.

My best advice: When in doubt, leave it out. And never laugh harder at your own joke than does the person you tell it to.

Inappropriate Apparel

Dress, I find, has less importance than most suppose—and fashion designers would have you believe. Of course, I'm biased by my belief that character, not clothes, makes the person. Most of us admire a snappy outfit. Our focus, however, rests on it but briefly. Then we become engaged with the wearer. Our goal is to relate to people rather than apparel.

The best way to dress is the way others will. The nature of the event usually dictates the level of formality. Within that level is a range. Even very formal events—black tie optional—leave a little room for personal discretion.

Over dressing can make you look like a show-off, under dressing like a bohemian. If you're unsure, err on the side of dressiness. You're less likely to draw untoward attention to yourself as the dressiest cat in the kennel than as the moron who mistook a presidential inauguration for a picnic. Who's that glue sniffing dude in the Lederhosen?

Women are more aware of dress than men. They tend to relish gowns in a way men do not take to tuxes. More important, they notice more about men's clothes than men do about women's. We gentlemen concern ourselves more with essentials, like what's under a woman's clothes. If it's members of the opposite sex you're out to impress, dress accordingly. The age of your intended "audience" is as important as its gender. An outfit that will wow ladies in their twenties may look ridiculous to those thirty years further down life's ambling path. Those of us who attended our 30th high school reunion and can still remember the tenth know whereof we speak.

The only absolute No-no is smelly clothes. Nothing compensates fully for a foul olfactory factor. Your firm grip, fine smile, and intent eye contact will fail to avail if you stink. If your nose is inured to stale perspiration clinging to the pores of your under or outer-wear, play it safe and wash them often.

Bad Breath

Nothing short of fresh buggers on your face turns people off faster than bad breath. It's insidious; we don't even know we have it. Few of our friends will tell us. Even our dentist may remain mum. So what do we do? Brush often and rinse before going out. Baking soda in warm water is more effective than commercial mouth washes for neutralizing the microbes that cause most bad breath.

Sometimes an empty stomach can produce gases that travel upward and befoul your mouth. Keep a little something in your tummy—but off your teeth—when you sally forth to impress the public.

Chapter Eleven:
Special Occasions

House Or Office Visit

When you meet someone at his or her house or place of business, bring a small gift. You can choose something as simple as a flower, loaf of bread, piece of wrapped candy, decorative candle, or greeting card.

The gesture means more than the object, unless you deliver a new car or the deed to some mountaintop property.

We all have reverential feelings about our personal space, be it our home or place of work. Even if we're dissatisfied with it and wish for something larger or lovelier, it's ours and we expect people to respect it. When you bring a gift you're saying, "You have honored me by letting me enter your space."

This advice applies not just to the first time you meet someone but also to all subsequent encounters at another person's place. Deepak Chopra recommends bringing a gift, beyond your rosy smile, every time you visit someone. Because that admonition is the only thing I remember from eight hours of his tapes, I regard it as important.

Following a visit to someone's place, especially if you received a meal or other special courtesy, send a thank-you note. Email may suffice; hand-written is better. As hand-written notes sink ever closer to extinction, their impact increases. When a casual acquaintance of mine lost his son, I sent my condolence on a decorative folding card. The gentleman later told me, "Your card was an oasis of beauty amidst a sea of faxes."

If you see an article you know would interest the person you visited, include it with the note—or send it later. That kind of consideration makes a lasting impression.

Anytime you attend someone's party a thank-you is in order. A phone call will do, though a note is better. Think how you'd feel if you put on a party for fifty and got phone calls thereafter from all of them. The disruptions might discourage you from ever entertaining more than two people at a time.

Job Interviews & Sales Calls

Everyone knows the importance of appearing neat so I won't belabor it. What many people don't appreciate is the need to be informed about the position you seek and the company offering it. Are there things in the job description that didn't appear in the ad? Do any of them challenge you unduly? Do you have special skills that would strengthen your candidacy? What possibilities exist for advancement? In what areas does the company experience problems? Of what accomplishments is the company most proud?

To get this kind of information read the annual report. It costs no more than a phone call to have one sent to you. You may want to visit the company prior to your interview and talk to people. It will give you both facts and a feel for the company culture—employee morale, leadership style, policy, benefits, and working conditions.

Orvel Ray Wilson, author of *Guerrilla Selling*, tells a story about a woman who spent a day hanging around the loading dock of the company to which she'd applied for a job. She talked to delivery drivers and dock loaders. At her interview a week later, she outlined a plan whereby the company could save $200,000 a year — and went to work there at once. Knowledge is power. Have a lot and make it known.

Look for ways to connect with your interviewer. See if he or she has photographs, trophies, art objects, or mementoes from which you can infer interests. If you share one of those interests—sewing, sailing, putting, or parenting—compare experiences.

If you're willing to put aside conventional notions of professionalism, you might like another device. Ask for a piece of paper or even to borrow a pen so you can take notes. This shows the importance you give to what the person has to say. When the paper or pen passes from his or her hand to yours, lightly brush the person's finger. This innocuous, gender-neutral touch creates connection at a subliminal level.

Above all, have a positive attitude. Never belittle a previous employer or competitor's product. Simply say the company you want to join offers greater opportunity for professional growth. You're eager to learn more about the business and make a significant contribution.

If you're selling something, acknowledge the merits of your competitors' goods or service—then describe the advantages of yours. A common obstacle is getting people and companies to switch vendors. If you find out—often just by asking—what their areas of dissatisfaction are, you need only show how buying from you will overcome those slow delivery or no refund woes.

Again, knowledge—and eagerness to implement it—are your most powerful allies. Fear not that you'll know so much you'll sound like a know-it-all. Display your knowledge in a matter-of-fact manner, without any hint of smugness. Ask the interviewer or prospective client what important information he or she can tell you. That makes the person feel like a partner—and important.

In Moments Of Need

Through a travel agency I bought an airline ticket for what I thought was a ten-day period—enough time to conduct a seminar in Mendocino, CA and visit friends in and around San Francisco. Imagine my dismay when the day before my intended return, I discovered my ticket was a weekend special, now expired and valueless.

The travel agency refused to take any responsibility. Said the unsympathetic agent who had issued it, "You should have checked it before you left." The airline personnel I pleaded with on the phone were equally callous. They said I'd have to buy another—one way, at full fare, with no advance-booking discount.

After a full and frustrating day of calls to other airlines and even bus companies, I had dinner with a cousin. He said, "Gary, just take it up with an agent at the airport. They have more authority than those flunkies on the phone."

Next day, armed only with my expired ticket, I entered the airport and addressed an agent. "Hello, Sonya," I said, having read her nametag, "I'm Gary." I reached across the counter and shook her hand. "Do you have a minute to hear a story?"

"OK," she said with a bemused smile.

"Forty years ago I took my first airplane trip—on your airline. In those days, it mattered not how much luggage you had but what it weighed. My bag was thirteen pounds overweight. The agent said, 'That will cost you another $26.' Then he looked at me, thought a moment, and said, 'Forget about it.' You've been my carrier ever since. Now I need another favor."

Before I could finish the story of the expired ticket, the agent, now beaming, handed me a boarding pass and said, "Have a nice flight, Mr. Michael."

Schmoozing got me on that plane. Schmoozing means talking with people in a positive way, visiting, connecting. A little schmoozing makes people more receptive. It gives them a chance to see you as a human being, especially one who sees them as human beings. In the public speaking seminars I teach, I stress putting connection before content, humanizing yourself to your audience before you regale them with your information and ideas. Schmoozing is the same thing at a person-to-person level.

When you find yourself in a pinch, schmooze. The hotel clerk tells you, "We have no rooms left." The cop says, "You made an illegal turn." The dry cleaner says, "We can't possibly have your suit ready this afternoon." Don't start bleating about your desperation. The clerk, cop, and cleaner have heard it all and don't care. If you get angry you'll only exacerbate the matter. Schmooze. It guarantees nothing but may save the day—or at least get you higher on the room waiting list, written up for a lesser violation, or your suit ready first thing in the morning.

Aye Jaye, a professional comedian and author of a book on schmoozing, has an extra ploy for police. He glued his donor's card to the back of his driver's license. On the card he wrote, "Take the genitalia too." In any stressful situation, the best schmooze is the one that brings laughter.

PART TWO

Authenticity In Everyday Life

Everything we've talked about so far comes under the heading of social graces. These techniques are useful because they put others at ease and make them feel important. Now we ask what end a good first impression serves. Ostensibly we want to make a good first impression to create a relationship and get it going in a positive direction. If the possibility of relationship doesn't exist, first impression skills are no more than polite practices with little or no long-term value.

As a relationship develops, social skills assume less importance and character counts for more. Character carries us beyond mere grace to substance. A person who has charm but no moral fiber soon wears thin. The best of first impressions not backed by sincerity will give way to disillusion. If your only aim in making a fine first impression is to manipulate other people—get them to hire you, buy from you, or sleep with you—read no further. If, on the other hand, you want your first impression skills to be an extension of your character and essential self, read on. The rest of the book is about ways to be more authentic.

Chapter 12:
What Is Authenticity?

"Identity is the artificial flower on the compost heap of time."
– Louis Menand

"Does it frighten us to discover how completely all that we are and do moves within the sphere of relativity? Perhaps it does, but this is precisely what we must discover."
– Karl Barth

The Self

We usually take authenticity to mean behaving in accord with our professed values. Expressions like "Walk your talk" and "He's his own person" reflect a consistency of action and word, as well as a personal value system rather than blind adoption of someone else's.

These expressions are fine as far as they go; they just don't go very far. Authenticity, I believe, incorporates much more than the mere absence of hypocrisy and having a personal set of values. It has a connection to a number of qualities and attitudes. It also embraces something we call truth, the specific truth of who we are individually and the general truth of what it means to be human. In short, we come to terms with our own reality.

That reality is elusive at best. While none of us doubt we have something we call our self, think for a moment about what the thing we call a self is. We undergo constant change. Few, if any, would defend the view that they are the same person they were ten years ago? We learn new things, even as we forget others. Our characters develop, we hope for the better. Our ideas change. The experience of aging itself is an agent of change. We acquire new responsibilities, take on new tasks, enter new relationships, and define ourselves, both to others and ourselves, in new ways.

Our bodies become less resilient. Cells die, joint spaces shrink, creases mark our once smooth faces, and maladies find us easier prey. And these changes occur gradually, often with such insidious leisure that they catch us unaware, until an off-hand glance in a mirror reveals a significant diminution of hair or expansion of girth that belies what we believed was a hiatus in, as Henry James called it, "a long, slow march into enemy territory."

So you probably agree that whatever it is we call our self is not a fixed thing but an ever-changing thing, really not a thing at all but a process. And because it's a process, we can only speak accurately about where it's been. Of where it's going we know only one thing with absolute certainty. And even of that, we know only the where, not the when.

Growth, flux, entropy — that's the arena in which what we call the self moves, lives and has its being. How, then, do we come to terms with our own reality? How do we obey the Socratic dictum "Know thyself," given the transient, ambiguous nature of that self?

Relativity Of Life

I think self-knowledge starts with accepting that our selves are just that — transient and ambiguous. We accept the relativity of life. By that I mean that the values we embrace we hold on faith rather than the basis of some demonstrable or universally agreed upon fact. We live without metaphysical guarantees for what we call truth.

We need also accept that the universe is not here to serve us. If it does, fine. But it is we who need to attune ourselves to it, not it to us. Stephen Crane put it succinctly in this poem:

A man said to the universe:

"Sir, I exist!"

"However," replied the universe, "the fact has not created in me a sense of obligation."

This indifference of our physical surroundings — The rain falls on the just & the unjust (Ecclesiastes) — seems especially true in matters of love. To give love may make receiving it more likely but does not assure that we will, and certainly not on the terms of our choosing. But that may be another subject.

Absence Of A Fixed Life Purpose

Another meaning of relativity is that life has no fixed meaning. Part of what it means to be authentic is recognition of one's inability to impose one's own meaning on others. Convinced as one may be that there is a God who has revealed the purpose of life to mankind, that we are to glorify him by becoming vessels of His will, authenticity entails tolerance of alternative views. Here are some other common examples of responses people give to the question: What is life's purpose?

1) To leave the world a better place

This popular view holds that we have a human obligation to work toward the betterment of the world. How we do this is our choice. It may be through the creation of things that others can enjoy, like literature, sculpture, or architecture. It may be the creation of charitable foundations, hospitals, or programs that benefit others. It may be via volunteer work of some kind. People who hold this view say they find service to others, even if just members of their immediate family, their most fulfilling activity. Few of us would deny that we derive a deep satisfaction from knowing we made a positive difference in the lives of other people, the animals with whom we share the earth, or our environment. However admirable the strong moral dimension to this view, many stop short of claiming that service is the purpose of life to which we all are called. Henry Thoreau put it well when he said, "I came into this world, not chiefly to make this a good place to live in, but to live in it, be it good or bad."

2) To realize our full potential

The fact that most folks have peculiar talents and abilities leads some to postulate that the purpose of life is the fullest possible development of our human potential. Failure to nurture our capacities is wasteful of our greatest resource – our selves. Whether we develop ourselves athletically, musically, intellectually, or personally, the important thing is to treat ourselves as a project. Through interaction, exploration, goal setting, and discipline we strive to become all that we can be. And in so striving, undeterred by our failures and never smug in our successes, we realize life's elixir.

3) **To school our souls for a life of pure spirit beyond the grave**

Many people regard our current life as a mere prelude to an eternal one. The purpose of this life is to prepare our selves for that to come. The rampant variety of ideas about the next life need not concern us here. Whether conceived as union with God or the blissful state of nirvana, the life beyond is the goal. The life we now have is so we can get ready. Very often that preparation entails forms of devotion and responsiveness to a source of meaning outside our selves.

4) **Self-awareness**

"...To venture in the highest sense is precisely to become conscious of oneself," said Kierkegaard. Although Kierkegaard held that such self-knowledge includes a relationship to God, others believe that one can become fully aware of his or her self apart from any theological context. Some even say that reference to a transcendent being blurs spiritual vision and hinders self-awareness. A strong inner life, whether based on study, meditation or ritual, suffices. Such a life usually includes rejection of control over others and embraces sympathetic insight into them and oneself.

One of the most interesting forms of this general outlook is that advanced by K. Singh. He taught that the purpose of life is to align our own energies with the longitudinal energy currents of the earth. This brings us into harmony with the world.

5) **Personal pleasure**

Shallow as the term pleasure may strike us, the fact is that most of us lead our lives as though this were our major motivation. We relish good food, entertainment, recreation, romantic engagement, and the company of friends and family. We pursue

happiness by maximizing enjoyment and minimizing discomfort. For some, pleasure is tranquility, the absence of worry. For
others, it is the life of the mind, learning new things or absorp-
tion in the imaginary worlds of film, theater, and fiction. Still
others prefer adventure, the intensity of emotional and physical
stimulation, adrenaline rushes from confronting new challenges.

Kurt Vonnegut suggests yet another meaning of life. He told
an audience I was part of about having gone out one day to get a
manila envelope to mail a manuscript to his publisher. He first
went to the office supply store, where he had to wait in line to
get the envelope. That gave him a chance to visit with neighbors.
Next stop was the PO, where he chatted with other waiters-in-line
till his turn came. The postal clerk, he said, is a well-endowed
woman, and he takes pleasure in admiring her amplitude. Upon
his return to home after an hour's absence, his wife said: "You're
not a poor man. You could buy a dozen, even a hundred,
envelopes at a time. Furthermore, you could buy a scale and
weigh your own manuscripts, then affix the appropriate postage.
Look at the time you'd save!" "Alas," said Vonnegut, my wife just
doesn't know what we're on earth to do. We're here for one reason: to fart around."

Whether you ascribe to one of these purposes of life, some
other we haven't mentioned, or a combination (they needn't be
mutually exclusive), you cannot make a rational, convincing
argument for the universal truth of your purpose as opposed to
someone else's. We can appeal to authorities like religious books
and wise people. We can proclaim that our own experience vin-
dicates the efficacy of a particular view. But we cannot compel
others to embrace our belief. In authenticity we recognize the
relativity of life, the presence of change and the limitations of
any human point of view.

Fallibility

Another way we accept our relativity is to confess our fallibility. Nietzsche said: "A very popular error: having the courage of one's convictions. Rather it is a matter of having courage for an attack on one's convictions!"

An important part of being authentic is having a self-critical capacity. Can we stand back and observe ourselves, not with absolute objectivity, for to suppose that our observation were absolutely objective would be a denial of the very fallibility it was designed to recognize. The idea is to hold our behavior up to the standards we have chosen and note the inevitable disparity. Without self-criticism there is no self-correction.

The authentic person can listen to the critical comments of others. He can then weigh them, if not objectively, at least honestly and acknowledge to what extent they have merit. He neither becomes immediately defensive nor searches for reasons to discount the criticism. In fact, he may welcome it as an opportunity to examine his behavior more closely and reshape it so as more fully to realize his own ethical goals for himself.

Dark Side

One aspect of our fallibility is what some call our "dark side." This may be the profoundest insight of both traditional Christian and modern psychological thought: Most of us are capable of some really awful acts, if not of body, surely of mind. Despite our good deeds and positive energies, each of us carries a measure of fear and insecurity, envy and resentment, regret and anger. To deny it is a lie and inauthentic. Jung put it more gently: "We do not become enlightened by imagining figures of light but making the dark conscious.

Recognition of our dark side is not just an ethical imperative of authenticity; it is also an imperative of psychic health. The psychotherapist Sidney Jourdard believes that we increase our self-knowledge itself in our attempts to make our whole self known to another. "...When a man does not acknowledge to himself who, what and how he is, he is out of touch with reality, and he will sicken. No one can help him without access to the facts. And it seems to be another fact that no man can come to know himself except as an outcome of disclosing himself to another person."

Jourdard points out the relation of disclosure to love. We risk exposure of our innermost self only if we feel that our audience is supportive and trustworthy. We want to know all we can about those we love. Allowing another to know us as fully as possible is an act of love. Self-disclosure is a way we permit others to love us. Exposure leaves us vulnerable. Once a weakness becomes known, people can exploit it for their own purposes. We reveal our vulnerability at our peril. Yet not to reveal it to anyone constitutes an even greater peril: that of losing touch with who, what, and how we are.

Fallibility & Point Of View

If we really take our fallibility seriously, you may ask, how can we ever take a stand on an issue? Knowing we could be wrong does not disqualify us from having a point of view. We can be acutely aware that we might be wrong in an opinion or moral stance, yet vigorously defend our position if it is heartfelt and based on available evidence.

Later we may decide we were wrong. The thing to do is to admit it, to yourself and others, rather than "stick to your guns" in hopes of salvaging the appearance of rightness and consistency.

Authenticity asks that we take ethical issues seriously, approach them with an open mind, and consider alternatives carefully before deciding one way or the other. It does not ask that we shirk from moral decision because we may later change our mind. Change, as we know, is part of life. The fact of change should be an antidote to dogmatism, not an excuse to avoid moral deliberation.

Chapter 13:
Authenticity & Philosophy

"What might the real me be like? How does it look, smell, taste?
How would I recognize it if I found it?"
– Robert Thurman

Some Philosophical Contributions

Let's look at what four philosophers have to say about what
it means to be human and an authentic self.

Sartre

Jean Paul Sartre held that people are free to choose their own
natures, to define themselves without reference to some pre-exis-
tent concept. No matter what our genes, upbringing or historical
situation, we always have choice over our response. Any attempt
to hide from that freedom Sartre called bad faith.   He urges us
to acknowledge our freedom and accept responsibility for how
we exercise it. In one sentence: "Man is nothing else but what he
makes of himself."

Bad faith is an attitude that takes the form of denial or self-
evasion. For example, prejudice is a kind of bad faith. Bigots
choose to blind themselves to facts.   Instead of letting
facts determine their ideas, they let prejudice determine what
they hold as facts. Their bigotry replaces thinking. It gives them
something "certain" to cling to and a cause to embrace. Denial is

implicit in their uncritical attachment to certainty, self-evasion in their unquestioning immersion in a cause. So strong is the human urge toward bad faith that results in prejudice, says Sartre, that "if the Jew did not exist, the anti-Semite would have to invent him."

Bad faith appears even in positive human relations. Often what we call love is merely attachment or, worse, emotional dependency. The more emotionally dependent we become, the more fiercely we proclaim our love. When we look to another to fulfill our humanity, we turn that person into an object, especially if we attempt in any way to possess the person. Possession, whether physical or mental, makes of the person a thing among things. As such, it is a denial of the person's freedom and humanity—a lie.

To be human, in Sartre's view then, means to be utterly free and totally responsible. One cannot take moral refuge in excuses like those of malevolent upbringing, racial discrimination, or financial need. He describes our radical freedom as a kind of condemnation. We don't create ourselves in the biblical sense of making something out of nothing; we are "thrown" into the world. But once there we are responsible for everything we do, even the ravaging torrents of passion on which we often seek to blame unseemly acts. Sartre says passion itself is an action, something we choose, and we "are nothing else than the ensemble of (our) acts, nothing else than (our) life."

Recent research into the development and functioning of the brain has brought data to light that suggests outside forces like childhood abuse or chemical imbalance can, in fact, determine aspects of behavior. Nevertheless, the thrust of Sartre's thought is still valid: We must hold ourselves accountable for our actions. This part of his philosophy challenges the culture of victimization in which people seek refuge from personal responsibility by blaming whatever bothers them on others.

Sartre says we are responsible for our past both because it was, in part at least, our actions that made it what it was and we are free to choose what meaning it shall have to our current projects. This theme of personal responsibility finds powerful articulation today in the person of a professional speaker named W. Mitchell. A motorcycle crash and explosion left him disfigured and fingerless. Later a flying mishap left him partially paralyzed. Mr. Mitchell's message, delivered from a wheelchair to audiences around the world, is simple, succinct, and very Sartrian: "It's not what happens to you that matters; it's what you do about it."

Buber

Another philosopher, Martin Buber, distinguished between two kinds of relationships: I-it and I-Thou. The former is the relation we have to things; they are objects for us. And in many of our dealings with other people, they, too, are objects in as much as we use them in some way. The use isn't necessarily manipulative; we simply see the other person as a means, an occasion for meeting some need of our own, even the need for love. Buber calls this "the exalted melancholy of our fate." An example is salespersons who see any person before them as a potential buyer. Such salespeople use first impression skills to ingratiate themselves to prospective customers—and closing techniques to clinch the sale. This doesn't make salespersons bad; it just means their job requires them to treat prospects as means, as "it's." Likewise, when we look to our loved ones to make us happy, we treat them as a means. Just because we reciprocate their love and contribute to their happiness doesn't alter the fact that a means-to-an-end dynamic invades the relationship.

The second kind of relationship, I-Thou, recognizes and honors the uniqueness of the other person. In no way is he or she an object, but a presence that confronts us as a whole personality, a Thou. Such relationships are both immediate and fleeting, fleeting precisely because it is impossible to live all the time in the present moment.

In the film "The Verdict," Paul Newman plays an attorney called upon to represent a woman who, having been given the wrong medication during a hospital stay, is left permanently comatose. He goes to the hospital to take photographs of her. For a while he clicks off exposures from different angles as though he were taking pictures of a table setting. Suddenly something strikes him. He pauses, puts down his camera, and stares at the unconscious figure before him. What had been a mere occasion for demanding a large judgment is suddenly a human being, a person, however reduced, a Thou. Then the epiphany passes. He picks up his camera and resumes his professional duties.

Our ineluctable attempts to organize our futures require that we perceive other people as means, objects, "It's." As Buber says, "Without It man cannot live. But he who lives with It alone is not a man." In other words, a real person, what we are calling authentic, is one who now and again can step beyond I-it into the realm of I-Thou. Said Buber, "All real living is meeting."

Marcel

Gabriel Marcel is similar to Sartre in emphasizing personal freedom and to Buber in insisting on the necessity of treating other people as ends, not means. His contribution to the subject of authenticity lies first, in his distinction between two kinds of truth. Scientific truth, he held, is wonderful and limited, wonderful because it is accessible to all and verifiable. Private, or subjective, truth, on the other hand, is inseparable from the inner struggle and spiritual development of the person to whom it belongs.

In other words, the truth that matters most to personal, existential reality, is a truth unavailable to disinterested investigation. This truth is not about the accurate description of observable fact. It is about overcoming spiritual emptiness and insensibility through the pursuit of illumination. Illumination is not a once-and-for-all kind of insight. It's an ongoing process of self-discovery and takes place only if we have the courage to face unpleasant as well as affirming truths.

Those familiar with Kierkegaard and Pascal will recognize Marcel's similarity to them. Both those earlier thinkers were keenly aware of the subjective nature of personal truth, the truth about our own being, our self. Marcel adds to their insights by pointing out the social dimension of self-understanding. He makes clear that the "I" only exists in the midst of the "We." Only by way of personal interaction do we attain our full humanity. Community is the arena in which authentic existence not only takes place but also flourishes.

Marcel believes in the worth of human personality. Our knowledge of this worth comes to us not by way of abstract doctrine, whatever the authority, but through direct awareness we have in communing with others. It is in personal encounters, our dealings with others, that we hear the call of conscience. Conscience is a call to self-discovery. To remain creative, or open, in the face of conscience, Marcel says we must relinquish all constricting assumptions that tempt us to put principles before persons. The vexing question of "Who am I?" is not susceptible to logical analysis. No one has the inner data to answer it, not even the person who asks. We view our own lives through the prism of the present, allowing who we think we have become to influence who we think we were. The sum of one's achievements and actions is conditioned by the reactions of other people. Who among them can decipher the "real person?" We are as mysterious to ourselves as to others, in this sense. Even though we may have a vague sense of purpose, we can't precisely define it.

Thus the matter of my identity—and with it the meaning of life—escapes my conscious grasp at any given time. We are strangers to our own depths. Our best hope, says Marcel, is to give up the pursuit of self-knowledge per se and move toward communal participation. Self-sacrifice, in particular, aids us in getting our life by letting go of it. By moving into shared ideas and feelings we can enter an intimacy that transcends self-consciousness. When we take on the joys and sorrows of others, we may experience grace, which includes the gift of our self.

Marcel's philosophy is a fierce challenge to the dehumanizing forces of contemporary civilization. Against all impulses that would reduce us to our specialized functions, job descriptions, and societal conditioning, he asserts that it is an honor to be a human being. What he wrote in 1952 still rings true today. "The first and perhaps only duty of the philosopher is to defend man against himself: ...against that extraordinary temptation towards inhumanity to which—almost without being aware of it—so many human beings...have yielded."

Plato

A much earlier writer by the name of Plato didn't use the word authentic but had his literary spokesman, Socrates, speak for most of a big book about justice, or that condition of the soul in which the three parts, appetite, spirit and reason, are in perfect harmony under the benign guidance of reason. The just person is the happy person because he or she is what, in today's lingo, we call integrated or centered. To achieve such justice, Plato further postulated, people had to organize themselves socially in a similar way, with a hardy working and a spirited warrior class guided by wise, benevolent rulers. For him, justice, or harmony, was as much a social as individual phenomenon. To fully realize their human potential people need a favorable social context. Plato's idea of harmony, what we often call balance, will prove valuable to our discussion of the elements of authenticity in the next chapter.

Chapter 14:

Elements Of Authenticity

"Every crime against one's own nature...records itself in our unconscious and makes us despise ourselves."
– Abraham Maslow

Harmony

Authenticity, as should be clear by now, is a complex concept with more to it than simply walking our talk.

Part of authenticity involves maintaining a modicum of Platonic harmony among the different impulses and facets of the process we call self. That doesn't mean we can't commit passionately to some priority and throw all of our energy at it for a time. It means that we accept, a la Sartre, that the value of the priority may stem from our having chosen it rather than some divine validation and that in choosing it we take responsibility for its outcome, including the "self," the moral entity, our choice helps to shape.

The harmony includes a recognition that we're complicated creatures with multiple dimensions to our self. To treat ourselves as though we were mere mind, body or spirit is to do violence to our totality. And authenticity means we accept that although we're products of our past choices and the circumstances they have created, we're always free to realize some new potential. That may mean letting go of old beliefs and habits, relinquishing part of our self-image in order to create ourselves in a new and unfolding one.

Other People As Ends

Authenticity also means treating other people as ends, not means. Even when we objectify other people in some way, as we inevitably do, we remain acutely aware that there is a realm of relating that transcends objectification. This is the realm of the profoundest intimacy, the greatest immediacy, the fully present Other that Buber calls I-Thou. And if we do not dwell from time to time in this realm, we diminish our humanity.

We recognize also that authenticity is not a solitary pursuit. As Marcel makes clear, it occurs only in the context of community. Authenticity is a way of behaving toward others. The self-knowledge it entails comes to us through our interactions with people around us. It is in relation to them that we find real freedom, a freedom in which our choices matter.

Accepting Our Differences

One way of treating other people as ends is to accept their difference from us, as we ask that they accept our difference from them. Just as authenticity requires us to become comfortable with who we are, to trust in our own impulses and urges, taste and values, it requires us to grant others the same freedom. That doesn't mean we have to approve, much less condone, cruel or greedy acts. It means simply that we allow others to make their own informed, rational decisions about what kind of person they want to become, what kind of process they are.

We can provide guidance—instruction through word and example. We can point out the unpleasant consequences of some kinds of actions. We can even take steps to protect ourselves from the harmful actions of others. All societies do this through their laws and the punishments for breaking them. We can incarcerate people and, in this country, even execute them. What we can't do is recreate others in our own image; to attempt to is presumptuous, a denial of individual autonomy, and inauthentic.

Even parents, whose role it is to give shape to their children's characters, have the task of letting go at some point and allowing the children to become their own persons. It's one of the hardest things a parent has to do and one of the most necessary. Just as a teacher serves a student ill if he keeps him forever a student, a parent does violence to a child when he treats him forever as an extension of himself.

We serve others well when we encourage them to blossom in their own way, to cultivate their uniqueness and become distinct individuals. The most rewarding aspect of my work as a professional speaker is the opportunity to help people feel OK about being who and how they are. I cherish the memory of a gentleman coming up to me after a leadership program and thanking me for having given him permission, as he put it, to be himself. He said, "I always thought you had to be dynamic, have a deep, melodic voice, and keep people laughing. You showed me that sincerity and caring for your audience are more important than delivery skills."

Gratitude

Another way to treat others as ends is through expressions of gratitude. When someone has done something nice for us, we can make sure they know how much we appreciate it. All too often favors, especially those performed regularly, get taken for granted. Some people seem to regard the continued perform- ance of such favors as an obligation, almost a divine right. That kind of callousness in the face of kindness is a sin against authenticity. He who commits it squanders an opportunity to treat his benefactor as a Thou. I think when we go a little further than usual in our thanks, when we write a note, send a gift, or make a call that shows not just gratitude but abundant gratitude, we reaffirm that other people are ends, Thou's, not just means.

Presence

To treat others as ends is to be fully present for them. In the first part of the book, we looked at presence as a social grace. Because ordinary conversation is the customary context for demonstrating presence, active listening is the best way to do it. In mainstream American culture, active listening means looking at the speaker, nodding or otherwise acknowledging that we are paying attention, asking questions about what has been said or requesting more information. To listen attentively is a difficult skill. We tend to think about what we want to say rather than concentrating totally on what someone else is saying. We become easily distracted by other activity around us, perhaps a television or other persons in the area. Our eyes wander. We fiddle with keys or a pencil, anything at hand.

Inner chatter makes us less present. We think about things that pre-occupy us, especially professional and domestic problems, rather than what someone is saying to us at the moment. This takes us away from the moment and limits our ability to respond genuinely, compassionately, and spontaneously. It leaves us less present and, hence, less authentic.

Active listening requires patience and discipline. One doesn't acquire the habit overnight. It's eminently worth the effort, however. Good listening is the single most effective communication tool we have. It's also a very powerful way to express recognition of other people as ends.

Forgiveness

Apologies may be the most difficult acts required of us in the name of authenticity. Our pride gets in our way. In disputes of all sorts, we want to maintain our rightness, especially if we are sincerely convinced of it. Arguments about who's right and who's wrong constantly creep into personal and professional relationships. To hold our ground, to articulately defend our position, goes a long way toward leaving us feeling justified. And we all like to feel justified, ethically correct. That's why it's such a bind: Other people feel the same way. We all want to be right.

Yet when we have wronged another, or even left another feeling we have wronged him, an apology is the best way to overcome the impasse. When we apologize to another person, even ask for forgiveness, we are treating him or her as an end. Ideally the apology is sincere. Otherwise, it may be just another attempt to manipulate a situation to our own advantage, to gain someone's goodwill for our own ends.

I think it's possible that even an insincere apology can serve authenticity. Everything depends on the intent. Suppose you and a friend are having one of those arguments that go back and forth. One person says, "You did..." The other counters, "But before that you did..." We've all had this kind of debilitating exchange in which each side seeks to blame the other for starting the problem. Suppose also that you really and truly believe your friend is at fault but you believe his interests, as well as yours, would be served by putting the debate behind you. Then, I think, you would do well to utter an apology so the friendship can get back on track. The apology is a kind of white lie; something said to save someone else's feelings rather than to flatter him in order to incur goodwill you can then turn to your advantage. The line gets thin at times, yet I believe it's the intent of an apology that governs its ultimate authenticity. At the very least, we should be honest with ourselves regarding our motive. Let us not delude ourselves that apologies uttered for our own sake make us more authentic.

To ask for forgiveness when you really believe it is the other party who should do so is a way of extending forgiveness. The extension of forgiveness, especially in the absence of a request for it, is a form of love and, hence, a profound expression that to you the person forgiven is a Thou. In a way, human freedom, one of the premises of our whole discussion, demands that we forgive each other. In Hannah Arendt's words, "Without being forgiven, released from the consequence of what we have done, our capacity to act would, as it were, be confined to one single deed from which we could never recover; we would remain the victims of its consequences forever."

Another premise of our discussion is that we're all both fallible and subject to the ambiguities created by the relativity of values. When we ask for forgiveness, we confess our fallibility and may very well prompt an authentic encounter.

Chapter 15:

Authenticity In Relationships

"...To have a self...is the greatest concession made to man, but at the same time it is eternity's demand upon him."
- Kierkegaard

Authenticity is a normative category. Authentic describes a commendable relationship to oneself and others. This relationship is an important part of what we call character, the extent to which we are "good" or "bad" people.

Authenticity is also a descriptive category. It suggests ways of understanding and developing our self that don't necessarily bear on character. Everything said here about authenticity and the self has implications for interpersonal relationships. Therefore it may seem silly to designate a chapter to authenticity and relationships, as though we could isolate the subject from what we've already talked about. Setting aside a chapter for this subject has much more to do with literary convenience than a discernible distinction in content.

My task as a writer is to get the ideas down as lucidly as I know how and leave it to you, the reader, to connect them in your own way. Authenticity is too personal, profound, and elusive a topic to fit into tidy compartments with clearly defined connections. And were I even capable of tying disparate chapters together into an elegant whole, I would undermine an important premise of my presentation: Life isn't like that.

Internalized Values

When I was growing up, my mother had a predictable response to every suggestion I ever made that ran counter to her sense of propriety: "But what will other people think?" No refrain was more often repeated in our household. It was not a question on my mother's lips; it was an objection. It meant she perceived my proposed action as inconsistent with social expectations. Only once did she even come close to demonstrating she regarded me as an autonomous person with his own values rather than as a reflexive rebel intent on embarrassing her. I expressed a view on some political issue that was mildly radical for the time and she said, "I know what you are. You're an idealist." Had I suggested I was about to take public action on my view, she would have said, "But what will people think?"

It was not our divergence of views that set us apart. Indeed, on many things we agreed. The chasm between us was that her value system was largely a function of what she thought other people thought, mine of what I thought, however meager my reasoning or faulty my view at the time seems in hindsight. Whether the difference had more to do with our childhood environments or genetic inheritance, I don't know. My mother lost her mother at an early age, was raised for a while by an aunt until her father remarried, and witnessed her father's business disintegrate and him become a pensioner at age thirty-five. As an adult, she sought psychiatric help for what then was called "insecurity." (Now we probably call it ego deficiency syndrome or some such thing.)

I grew up in a stable family environment, did not lose a parent until my adulthood, and saw my father advance through hard work. Whatever the reasons, I was determined from an early age to decide for myself the ideas and behaviors I would embrace. I wanted to be myself, whoever that might turn out to be, not a mirror of anyone else. My rebelliousness may have been for its own sake at times, as my mother never tired of pointing out, but it was a necessary step in the development of my own sensibility and value system. My mother, on the other hand, was in bondage to what she thought were others' "ought"s. I do not mean to imply she had no values of her own or was incapable of taking an unpopular stand. That would be untrue and an insult to her memory. I mean simply that her foremost value was to maintain an image of respectability within the community, and she found threatening any behavior on her son's part she thought others would deem less than respectable.

Literature is replete with stories of problems caused by people trying to impose their values on others, especially their children. Romeo and Juliet is the classic example. In Shakespeare's play, two feuding families can't abide the idea of one of their members marrying a member of the other. The result is tragedy. Goals go awry often enough when they are our own. When the goals are those of others, we're really outmatched. We're out of sync with ourselves, or more accurately, we haven't got much of a self. That means we're out of authenticity because to be authentic we must take charge of and become responsible for our own life. Being you is too important a job to be left to anyone else.

Acceptance

Since authenticity involves acceptance of our own fallibility, I think it implies acceptance of our uniqueness. We don't have a

Model Man or Woman to pattern ourselves on. We create our own model using the resources available to us — inherited wisdom, parental and societal training, intuition, and reason. No model is perfect, and we never perfectly realize even our imperfect models. As we come to terms with our imperfection, we do the same with our uniqueness and that of others. Put paradoxically, we become secure, or at least comfortable, with our insecurity. We give ourselves permission to share our vision with others and do not become frustrated when they cling to their own. That's a difficult, maybe impossible, task when we are firmly convinced of our rightness. Until we accomplish it, however, we have not fully come to terms with our fallibility, the fact that we are a process, or the relativity of life we discussed earlier. We have not become fully authentic.

Fallibility means we can't always be right, that truth often eludes us. Some people flee from their fallibility by taking dogmatic stands on every imaginable subject. "I don't know" and "I'm not sure" aren't part of their vocabulary. People who accept their fallibility show more comfort with uncertainty. They are not only less likely to confuse their wishes with reality; they tolerate a higher degree of ambiguity. While they may "yearn for an enduring world," to use Nietzsche's phrase, they have made peace with the fact that it's a utopian notion. We are in a constant state of becoming and transcend change only in death, if then. Universal values exist only in the minds of bygone philosophers, and even if every living human being agreed on a hierarchy of values, we'd find conflict on how to interpret them in specific situations. To the extent we can stand undaunted before the unknown, even welcoming it as an opportunity to learn something new, especially about our self, we nourish our authenticity.

Beyond Facades

It follows from this that, when we are authentic, we step out from behind our facades. We trust our self to be who we really are at that time. It doesn't mean that if we feel anger we're obliged to act it out; it suffices to admit to it. Of course, there are situations in which even an admittance of anger works against us. Suppose someone you hope will hire or buy from you fails to keep an appointment. If you mention how it angered you, you may put the person on the defensive and bust the deal. To get along in the world, we often have to decide between an honest expression of negative feeling and some end. We have no guidelines to tell us which course to take when. The person who feels compelled, in the name of candor, to disclose every negative feeling that casts its shadow on his soul may be more self-indulgent than authentic. The person who forever hides or denies his negative feelings for even a laudable reason, like getting along, sacrifices his authenticity on the altar of cheap peace. What makes the peace cheap is that it is founded on an illusion and may, if it crumbles, disappear completely.

Here's an example. A woman I knew accepted my invitation to meet me at an exotic locale, where I was to conduct a workshop. I told her I'd happily pay half her airfare, comp her on the workshop, and take care of our lodging. She asked that I also buy all her meals. The request struck me as extreme; we have to eat wherever we are. Since the cost to feed a woman for three days wouldn't break the bank and I was eager to be with her, I agreed.

We hit it off well. Her company transformed what would have been routine workdays into an intense romantic experience. When I started to write a check to her for what we had agreed on, she said, "Would you...uh...round it off." "Which way and why?" I asked. "Up to the next hundred dollar mark," she said, "I had some other expenses — long distance calls, transportation from the airport, and because of flight connections, I'll have to spend a night in a hotel on the way back."

Her request seemed fair. It went beyond the terms of our agreement but was within the spirit of it. I'd have felt better if she'd said, "I know what we agreed to but wonder if you'd mind paying half of some unanticipated expenses I incurred to get here." That would have been straightforward and not smacked of manipulation. Alas, I was wonder-struck by the woman and didn't want to put the good vibrations we were enjoying in jeopardy by raising an objection. So I gave her the extra money.

During the three-and-a-half days we were together, we visited two museums. For neither did she suggest paying her own way. When I paid, thinking again that the cost was too trivial to make it an issue, she didn't even thank me. She seemed to regard it as her divine right to be treated to everything. I thought her attitude was symptomatic of a serious character flaw, especially in light of her self-representation as a liberated, independent businesswoman. Again I said nothing for fear of disrupting the romantic joyride. And my silence was as inauthentic as her monetary predations.

When next we met, in yet another city, I refused to pay more than my agreed upon share for anything. This enraged her and she sabotaged the relationship. The details are ugly but unimportant to my point. By masking my feelings during our first rendezvous, even for what seemed at the time a decent reason, I contributed to the collapse of the friendship as surely as she did with her greed. Had I confronted her, it may well have ruined the mood, maybe even turned her against me. It might also have led to the kind of understanding that would have made for a firmer friendship than one fueled primarily by passion. At least it would have been authentic and probably precluded the painful circumstances of our reunion. My facade of acceptance encouraged her unsavory behavior and aided me in fooling myself that things would be better next time.

I believe we serve our own and others' interests best when we look for what's right about people. Ignoring what's wrong when it blatantly appears, however, is a form of denial and a ticket to trouble. Wanting things to be a way they are not is natural. Believing they are other than they are in the face of clear and unambiguous evidence is willful distortion, a kind of lie, and inauthentic.

Does this mean we have to act on all our feelings? No. As rational adults we can choose when to let our ire simmer. We can hold back so as better to serve a long-term goal, e.g., rapport, instead of venting. Most of us, even the most circumspect, sometimes hit a point where we feel that further patience will cause us internal anguish and constitute a denial of ourself. Then it's time to express how we really feel. I've been at that place many times. I regret only slightly that I did not extend my tolerance a little longer. I regret greatly that I framed so many of my expressions as accusations instead of just staying with my feelings. Of course, we always chance that even a tactful, non-accusatory expression of how another person's actions have affected us will be perceived as aggressive. To be in a relationship at all is to be at risk.

Unexpressed anger puts us at far greater risk than that we suppress. Unexpressed anger may come out indirectly, through complaint or bad mouthing to third persons, or clandestine acts of sabotage intended to undermine our offender. Given no outlet, unexpressed anger simmers within. The effect is toxic. It distracts you, leaves you with fantasies of revenge, and postpones the kind of direct confrontation that is necessary for the anger to dissipate. Remember: It's in your best interest to get beyond your anger. It can kill you. A direct expression of resentment that is specific about your feelings and what gave rise to them is authentic because it is honest.

Dealing With Our Dark Sides

I spoke earlier of the dark side we all have and how to deny it is inauthentic. Simply to admit, however, that we all have a dark part to ourselves isn't really adequate. True acceptance of our dark side means that we look at the ways it manifests itself and how the manifestations affect, usually infect, our relationships.

One way the dark side ambushes us is self-delusion. We'd all like to think we're nice people, full of love. We rarely, if ever, get angry. When we do, we never take it out on others. We're too evolved for that, too spiritual. Not only does it take psychic energy to maintain this fiction, we often project our unseemly qualities and emotions onto others. We end up hating in others something we bear in ourselves but don't dare acknowledge. (See Intimacy Section)

How, then, can we become more aware of our shadows? One way is to force ourselves to listen to the feedback of others. People close to us can tell us things about ourselves we naturally overlook. To listen to negative perceptions about us and not get defensive is a difficult task, yet maybe one of the most necessary in our quest for authenticity.

Two days before writing this section, I sat with a friend talking about the ways we push each other's buttons. She helped me realize that some of the less flexible stances I take, lines I draw in the sand, are fear reactions to a perceived threat to my autonomy. The fear stems from a childhood disdain for my father's inability to stand up to my domineering mother. Ironically, I had been allowing my mother to control my behavior as surely as she dictated my father's. My past held me captive.

It was a painful insight, but without it I had no chance of stopping the reflexive pattern. Now I feel better able to respond from a place of freedom. A person close to me raised my consciousness of my shadow. That's one of the things real friends are for.

Intimacy

No other form of love demands more of our authenticity than an intimate relationship. Intimacy puts us face to face with all the flaws—greed, insecurity, jealousy, resentment, etc.—that constitute our fallibility. At the same time it forces us to summon our nobler traits—patience, gentility, courage, and self-sacrifice. In an intimate relationship we find out more about ourselves than in a lifetime of introspection. We learn about our insecurities, weaknesses, and angry areas. We learn also about our emotional resources and capacity for caring. Intimacy is the ultimate revelatory experience, our fiercest confrontation with our humanity.

To attain intimacy requires trust. We dare to be who we are, pretending nothing, hiding nothing, and allow the same for our partner. We talk freely about ourselves—our fears, aspirations, and emotional needs. We're honest about what we like, what we can tolerate, and what we won't suffer. We accept the same from our partner without trying to change or convert that person. Such acceptance is difficult. Most of us are committed to our values and defend them vigorously. Our commitment may have congealed into entrenchment, in which case, we aren't candidates for intimacy. We lack the necessary flexibility to accept fully someone who doesn't share them. When being right is more important than being loved, intimacy is impossible. What Kenneth Tynan called "the tough, durable wires of sympathy" cannot develop. Intimacy, like authenticity, asks that we subordinate the very values that help define us to the experience of loving partnership. We need not stop being who we are; we need only sign off on trying to make our partner like us.

Another dimension of intimacy is sharing. Intimate partners share not in hope of reciprocation or enhanced image but for the sheer joy of sharing. They share what they have and who they are, for that is the task and comfort of love. Part of such sharing is taking some responsibility for each other's progress along the path of love. While each of us is ultimately responsible for his or her own spiritual development, intimate lovers serve each other as helpmates. They commend generous acts and point out behavior that lacks loving intent. They journey together and find in each other's blossoming their own.

This kind of love isn't something you can choose the way you would a mate, pet, or house. Intimacy is having an open heart and allowing ourselves to be vulnerable over an extended period. It develops slowly, through shared experience, accumulating on a foundation of friendship like moss on a rock. It doesn't lend itself to measurement but reveals itself in the ordinary rhythms of communal life. This sets it apart from romance, that blissful

excursion from mundane reality that first deludes then disillu-
sions the unwary. Intimacy rarely occurs during the first blush
of love; it tends to develop when romance fades.

Romance is about how we feel. Intimacy is about how we
are. It's both less intense and more encompassing than
romance. It's a place of rest because a shared life is a spiritual homeland. It's also an arena of uncertainty because we're
forced to confront our dragons, not knowing if we will prevail
against them. Romance is but foreplay to intimacy's true union.
This does not mean it cannot provoke romance, it often does.
Allowing ourselves to be vulnerable and open often elicits a loving response. The point is, confusing romance with intimacy
fails to grasp the complexity and depth of the latter.

Relationship is a risky enterprise and no place for those who
can't live with insecurity. Intimacy requires us to let go of our
assumptions about what relationships are supposed to be like
and to commit to a long-term program of discovery—about our
self, our partner, and what we can create together. It's an ongoing initiation into what I earlier called the relativity of life. Of
all human endeavors, no other can tell us so much about our
potential and our limitations. In relationship we come most
profoundly to know our self, who we are.

Albert Camus believed crisis reveals character. We don't
really know what people are like until we see how they react to
adversity. Pressure, deprivation, threat, and other insults to
body and mind show our true mettle. Anyone who has had a
legal, medical, or personal crisis may tell you: "I found out who
my real friends are."

Relationship, while not a crisis as such, is a decidedly crisis-like
situation. It's fraught with uncertainty, and uncertainty fosters
fear. Relationship forces us to come to terms with fear, to face it

or fold. Can we continue loving in the midst of fear? Can we stay loyal when the intensity of passion has faded and disillusion rears its frightful head?

So much for what intimacy is. Now how do we realize it? My ideas come from reflection on my experience, including reading and conversation with people who share my interest in the subject. I have an impressive record of relationship failures, and from them I've learned a few things.

If intimacy comes down to a single trait, or behavioral pattern, it's honesty. Dishonesty is not fatal to love. Intimacy, however, cannot survive dishonesty. Deception of any kind closes the open channel between partners that is the lifeblood of intimacy. When we hide something, part of our life is made unavailable to our partner. If we conceal either a thought or an action for fear of how it might affect our partner's perception of us, we put our image before the health of the relationship. In Buber's terms, we make of our partner an "It." If the motive for our secrecy is a reluctance to hurt the other person, we have probably done something for selfish reasons and feel shameful about it. The moral: Don't do what you can't talk about. As Brad Blanton says, "There is no such thing as 'none of your business' in and intimate relationship."

While honesty is essential, if it is not clothed in compassion it can become destructive. Truth hurled in someone's face with an attitude of "Here it is; deal with it" undermines intimacy. Let truth be your standard and kindness your guide.

I have a friend who has been married to the same woman for thirty years. They have an open marriage; sleeping with other people is permitted, even blessed. Because this arrangement is agreeable to both, it works. Granted, they are unusual people, seemingly untouched by the middle class toilet training that brain damages so many of us. They buck the cultural norm, the ingrained notions about what a marriage is supposed to be, to create their marriage according to a shared ideal. Shared is key: If either did not embrace sexual permissiveness as a personal and marital privilege, their relationship would have crashed long ago.

Whether intimate partners are sexually faithful to each other is important only if they have so agreed. Being honest with each other is always important. Part of honesty means clarifying expectations on both sides. Assumption is the mother of misunderstanding. Misunderstanding leads to feelings of betrayal. If you don't know—and you care—ask. Not asking is as dishonest as not telling, maybe more dishonest if it's more your issue than your partner's.

In one of my failed relationships, I justified, to myself, my repeated sexual excursions: "We have no formal agreement, so I'm not really being unfaithful." It was a self-serving excuse— and a sin against intimacy. It put me in a position of having to lie because I knew my partner would not be pleased if she knew what I'd done. What she doesn't know won't hurt her, I reasoned, like so many before and after me. Yet in a way it hurt us both because in deceiving her I put up a psychological barrier. I had to hide part of who I was, the very opposite of the openness intimacy and authenticity ask of us.

Honesty comes into play in another way. If we cannot honestly face our own shadows and recognize them for what they are, we will forever project them onto others. Vanity, not sex or power, is the most pervasive of human impulses. We all want desperately to think well of ourselves. Rather than take hard looks at our inner dragons, we prefer to make excuses or find justifications for our less seemly deeds. One of the most insidious ways we do this is to find in others the very character flaws that plague us.

Projection is a kind of coping device. By transferring blame we can preserve our self-regard. To deny a character trait like anger or selfishness is easier than eradicating it. In many areas of our life it works. Our involvement with other people isn't close or prolonged enough for it to matter, especially if we have redeeming features. Friends may choose to overlook anger if its manifestations do them no personal harm and they adore your wit and charm. However, a tendency to ascribe our own negativities to others is particularly treacherous in close relationships, especially intimate ones. When we refuse to acknowledge our dark side to a partner, the partner experiences it as a lack of intimacy. At heart, it's a refusal to be vulnerable, and without vulnerability intimacy can't occur. Yes, we have to contain our negative feelings much of the time; civility requires it. Containment is an adult process. Denial of the feelings is what gets us in trouble. Feelings don't go away. They hang around at a suppressed level and continue to affect our behavior. Recognizing them is the first and biggest step in coming to terms with them. Only when we see them for what they are, namely our own, can we stop projecting them onto others. We may never fully rid ourselves of them. Failure to see them for what they are can cause us more problems than the emotions themselves.

In an intimate relationship projection is deadly. It contradicts the open, honest nature of a relationship. It leads us away from vulnerability and into self-protection. It is a festering lie. That's why a person who does not know himself may never experience intimacy. We can't share fully if we we're in an emotional coma or we sport psychic armor that shields us from self-awareness.

For an intimate relationship to succeed, both partners need to express and receive feelings. If we're out of touch with our feelings, we can hardly express them. If we saddle our partner with our shadow side, either by attributing ours to them, or by blaming them for things we don't like about ourselves, we share less than our whole self. We also make it more likely that we will receive their feelings through a filter clouded by preconceptions and judgments stemming from our unacknowledged shadow.

Intimacy is about knowing ourselves as more than our roles, even the most vital, like those of child, parent, mate, and friend. In becoming more aware of yourself, you are more fully present—for yourself and others. You give yourself the best chance both to lose yourself in the larger reality of love and claim your authentic self.

The ideas we looked at in Part One are helpful in getting a relationship off to a good start. A good start creates comfort and opens the possibilities of rapport and lasting friendship. The deeper we want to go in a relationship, the more revealing we need to be. Some unease usually attaches to the process. If we own the unease and welcome it as an impetus to self-discovery, we give ourselves the best chance to advance toward intimacy. Part of the discomfort comes from finding out how our actions, habits, and mindsets affect others; yet until we do we operate blindly in an arena that calls for utmost clarity.

Besides honesty, intimacy requires total dedication—from both partners. Any kind of holding back, on either partner's part, undermines the intimate nature of the relationship. No one can coerce a partner into commitment. Only where love already exists is the soil fertile enough to nourish intimacy. Those who talk about intimacy while resisting maximum closeness won't be swayed by pleas or reason. Only people who want intimacy badly enough to pay the price—in the hard work of relationship and the hurts that come with it—will ever experience it. Nothing short of two persons' passionate devotion will bring intimacy about.

When you open yourself to another, allowing yourself to be vulnerable, the sharp words or inconsideration that inevitably arise between two imperfect beings cut deeper than similar slights from persons in whom you have less invested. Stresses, tensions, disagreements, and different degrees of emotional availability at a given moment are inherent in any relationship. No fits are perfect. Mighty as is the love we feel, we often fail to manifest it. One result is a measure of disillusion. How we handle disillusion is a major indicator of the course of a relationship. If you retreat at the first sign of disillusion, you short-circuit your glorious intention.

In a paradoxical way, pain is a prerequisite for intimacy. It puts you in touch with your vulnerability and an important part of who you are. It reveals to you and your partner your most tender parts. It is a way of shedding defenses and naive expectations so as to know your self in a new way. John Wellwood says in *Journeys of the Heart*: "When our heart breaks out of the protective shell we have built around it, and we shed our ideal images of how a relationship should be, we may feel naked. Yet in this nakedness we taste the essential nature of our existence. The truth is that we have no ultimate control over what happens to us in this life. Therefore, to feel naked and vulnerable is to be in direct contact with reality."

Being authentic means embracing reality, especially the truth about your self. The pursuit of intimacy forces you to face your spiritual resources and limitations as nothing else does. It holds up to you your level of loyalty, empathy, and compassion. It also forces you to confront your shadows, those character deficits and exposed nerves that mark you as a flawed, finite being. To fall short of intimacy—or even less profound forms of love— does not make a person inauthentic. The recognition that one is commitment phobic is actually authentic because honest.

Authenticity describes a relationship to truth, most of all the truth about our selves. Intimacy's significance for authenticity is its unparalleled power to reveal such truth, especially one's capacity for that most majestic of all human endeavors: love.

Forgiveness

I've spent more time pondering forgiveness than any other expression of love. No other act save self-sacrifice demonstrates love as profoundly and emphatically as forgiveness. Many couples' counselors consider it the single most important ingredient in a healthy marriage. I talked about asking forgiveness in the chapter "Elements of Authenticity." Now let's look at it from the side of him or her who grants it, because that person faces a critical decision.

Most of my ideas about forgiveness came from the biblical example of Jesus. He went around forgiving people, quickly and on the sole condition that they repent. Repentance consisted of recognizing one's offense and asking for forgiveness. The offended person had no moral choice other than to grant the plea for pardon—"seven times seventy seven times" if need be.

Much as I admire the ideal Jesus set before us, I think it fails to take account of our "fallen" natures. We aren't saints, just ordinary mortals saddled with all kinds of psychological baggage. We are selves in process. Any realistic discussion of forgiveness needs to address our unsettled natures. Forgiveness, no more than love itself, is something that happens all at once and completely. It more likely takes place over time and may never be total. It starts with a decision and becomes a project. Forgiveness doesn't mean negative feelings just disappear or we forget the injury done to us. Psychological injuries may never heal altogether. Some negative feelings may linger for life. Nor does forgiveness imply that we, as forgivers, have no right to expect anything in return.

You may say that any condition attached to forgiveness undermines its spirit. We should give it not on the basis of someone's attitude and behavior but because we choose to. Like God's love, which is always available, real forgiveness is unconditional. By giving it unbidden, we participate in a larger, even ultimate, reality.

I cannot disagree with this argument, especially the way my editor, Erika, articulates it. We spent an afternoon exploring the whole idea of forgiveness. Part of my discomfort with the insistence on unconditionality is personal: I simply find it easy to forgive those who ask for forgiveness and impossible to forgive those who make no gesture toward apology and healing the hurt they've brought.

Another part is philosophical. We are talking about forgiveness as a factor in authentic relationships. In cases where an injury goes undisclosed, some authenticity has already been sacrificed. If I wound you in some way and you don't tell me how my offense affected you, you have denied me the opportunity to see my action through your eyes and decide for myself what response to make. Neither of us has confronted an important truth, namely that something I did caused you pain. Even if we both know it but say nothing about it for fear of making things worse, our evasion strikes me as inauthentic.

In a case where I wound you and immediately disappear from your life, you may choose to forgive me but your choice has no tangible effect on our relationship. We no longer have one. You may feel better, even proud of your ability to forgive and closer to God, whose love you seek to emulate. Your inward action does not, however, touch me. Neither the purity of your motive nor the nobility of your decision enhances our non-existent relationship.

What I feel myself struggling to flesh out is an idea I heard years ago as a divinity student. *Grace is free but not cheap.* He who accepts the gift of grace—or forgiveness—accepts also his need for it and responsibility for reforming the behavior that created such need. Therefore, we do not give forgiveness the way we would a box of chocolates — to say "Thank you," show affection, or just on a whim.

Some people claim we forgive others not for their sake but our own. If we hang on to our anger, we punish only ourselves by harboring a clenched fist in our heart. Anger, to be sure, is a debilitating emotion. But there's a difference between clinging to, even cultivating anger and refusing to forgive. Our peace of mind depends on putting anger behind us (so much easier said than done!). It does not, however, require that we absolve those who have harmed us. While we may seek reconciliation, reconciliation for its own sake, with no foundation of earned forgiveness, may lead to resentment down the road. So-called expedient forgiveness lacks authenticity. It more likely merely suppresses anger than dissipates it. Suppressed anger is an emotion as insidious as jealousy. When it rears its head, it seethes.

Two considerations may help us enlarge our capacity to forgive. One is the knowledge that even when we think we've given our best, we may have inadvertently harmed someone. And we don't always give our best. Impatience, insensitivity, or selfishness get in our way time and again. We never banish our shadows; we can only try to deal with them and hope others forgive us when we fail. How often we are called upon to forgive is probably how often we are in need of forgiveness ourselves.

The second consideration is that no matter how blatant or unprovoked an injurious act against us seems, we may be part of the problem. Something in our behavior may have played a role in what happened. Authenticity demands that we examine what that role may have been and hold ourselves responsible for it. Fault is rarely unilateral, much as the aggrieved may wish to think so. This is another aspect of what I call the relativity of life. Jean Paul Sartre went so far as to suggest that we choose many of our emotions. Indignation, in particular, said Sartre, is something we muster in order to feel morally superior. I think the large numbers of people claiming "victimization" in our current culture lends credence to this notion.

In a perfect relationship, the need to forgive would never arise. Because no relationship is perfect, we make a conscious choice to release the perpetrator of an injustice from further judgment, to put aside our resentment and desire for retribution, and let healing begin. We neither annul nor sugarcoat the offense. Instead we recognize it as part of the ebb and flow in the life of any relationship and agree to move forward rather than dwelling on what cannot be undone. We acknowledge the reality of the injury but accept the contrition of the person who caused it as sincere and make room for another chance.

This kind of forgiveness is authentic because it takes account of the relativity of life, including the imperfection of all our relationships and moral judgments. It also acknowledges that all of us inflict injuries on others and, therefore, stand ourselves in need of pardon. Without forgiveness, love is doomed. Without love, few of us would find much to live for.

Granted, some offenses are so heinous and unjustified, like a murderous assault on a stranger, that forgiveness seems impossible. Acts motivated by jealousy or greed may be less brutal but they are still far reaching in their impact on the person sinned against. When a perpetrator refuses to acknowledge a wrongdoing or persists in his or her sinister behavior, forgiveness is very difficult.

In such cases, I can only suggest a course that stops short of forgiveness but may enable hurt persons to heal. With luck and effort, for our own sake alone, we can let go of the wound. The luck I have in mind is sometimes called grace. It's a gift we can ask for but not command. If blessed to receive it, letting go frees us from the pain of nursing a grudge and forever re-experiencing the injury. Letting go is damage control, an antidote for the kind of fermenting anger that can turn into bitterness. Ongoing bitterness threatens both our emotional and physical well-being.

No sanctimony attaches itself to mere letting go. We do not put our self in the place of God. Nor do we have to overcome the typical obstacles for forgiving. One is the comfort we find in the victim role, especially the sense of moral superiority it gives us. Another obstacle is that the offender may not ask for, or even deserve, forgiveness. Another is that we're reluctant to look critically at who we are and any possible responsibility we may have for the calamity. To let go we simply decide that an obsession with our injury will corrode our heart and leave us in permanent distress. Therefore, to help ourselves heal, we put resentment over the wound behind us.

The process isn't easy. It may take a long time and the help of a trained counselor. We let go to unburden debilitating baggage and open to a fuller, more loving life. We forswear vengeance and leave forgiveness to a higher power. It's freeing, and it's enough.

Chapter 16:
Authenticity & Spirituality

"The greatest thing in the world is to know how to be one self."
- Montaigne

Spiritual and spirituality mean different things to different people. To some they have a specifically religious connotation. Spirituality is the subjective side of religion, the sense of connection to God, or ultimate reality, brought about by belief and practice.   To others the words suggest the peace attained through meditation on or communion with the divine, however conceived. (The various ways people have defined the divine, from the biblical idea of a creator and lawgiver, to Buddhist thinking about a universal consciousness, to transcendentalist and New Age notions of a godly quality in everyone, could fill another book.)

Use of "spiritual" has become so common, and loose, that every time I hear an experience described as spiritual, I wonder if it's for lack of a better word or better experience. You, too, have heard friends refer thusly to activities as diverse as hiking in an especially splendid area, reading something that moved them emotionally, making love to one's beloved, or attending a worship service. Last week, a friend of mine reported having had a profoundly spiritual experience when he witnessed a total eclipse of the sun.

The common thing in these and other allegedly spiritual

experiences is the element of depth, of having been touched at some deep and not totally explicable level. When we feel ourselves in touch with something vital to our humanity, we tend to call it spiritual. That something both nourishes us and helps us to feel connected to a larger reality—God, nature, true self, love, humanity, etc. Paul Tillich called such reality the "ground of our being."

I want to talk about spirituality in the context of authenticity, especially as it relates to our awareness of self. As we've seen, much of authenticity has to do with knowing ourselves in the sense of what it means to be human and how we respond to our flawed, finite, ambiguous, transient nature; in short, how we utilize our freedom to shape who we are during the unending process of becoming.

Authenticity, then, is about truth. It demands that we understand what truth is, both for and about us, and come to terms with it. As such, it is a spiritual journey that leads us ever deeper into the most nagging, and perhaps mysterious, reality we confront—our self.

Idols

From a spiritual perspective, idolatry is the root of all inauthenticity. Idolatry, the worship of false gods, sets us on paths that lead away from self-understanding and creative unfolding toward arrested development and mindless repetition of old patterns; in short, stuckness.

Some idols are easy to spot, like money, fame, or power. Most of us have a weakness for one or more of these. I, for one, crave fame. Whether my ravenous desire for recognition stems from too little of it as a child or having been an only child for the first eight years of my life, psychologists can debate. The fact remains; I'm out of balance, not in harmony with myself. A reason for writing this book—though mercifully not the only reason—is to achieve more notoriety. If I wanted the notoriety simply because it would translate into dollars, which would enable me to enjoy a more interesting lifestyle, that would be, in my mind, within the bounds of acceptable ambition.

But I want notoriety and approval for their own sake; the attention of others has a terminal value for me. I thrive on it and feel deprived in its absence. This praying at the altar of a false god, as it were, is a spiritual flaw and sin against authenticity. Without recognition, I don't quite feel real. What an insidious form of vanity!

Other idols are harder to see, like goodness, values, and spirituality itself. An obsession with one's own goodness, or virtue, is still an obsession with an aspect of self. As such, it puts a person at risk of narcissism, a form of self-worship. There's an idol for you.

We also fall prey to value worship. Not that I think values are bad, or even that some aren't better than others. Values are part and parcel of consciousness. To think is to make determinations about what is good, less good, and not good at all. In the biblical story of creation, God did just that. He surveyed what he had created for each of six days and "saw that it was good."

When, however, we become so enamored with our values that we forget they too are part of life's relativity and may require periodic revision, we have made of them an idol. When we use our values to disparage all people who do not share them, we claim for ourselves a position of moral superiority. That superiority can become one more mind-calcifying attempt to grasp an absolute, one more idol.

We see this clearly in the debate over abortion. Proponents on both sides vilify each other. They assert that theirs is the only correct moral choice. Anti-abortion forces call those who want the procedure kept legal murderers. The very term "pro-life" implies that any other decision favors death. Pro-choice advocates accuse those who would ban abortion of wanting to deny a woman's sovereignty over her own body. They suggest that anyone opposed to abortion has no regard for personal freedom.

To hold a value and defend it passionately is not idolatrous. To suppose that others, who are neither ignorant nor immoral, could not choose differently is value worship. In religious language, it's putting oneself in God's place. The hardest moral decisions are those that require us to choose between competing values. Where the choice has drastic consequences, the decision should prove heart rending. A lapse into comfortable moral allegiance denies either the seriousness of the decision or the fallibility we bring to all decisions. It's a denial of reality and inauthentic.

Spirituality, if pursued as an end in itself rather than a vehicle of greater awareness, wholeness, and openness, can also become an idol. We may want to think of ourselves as "spiritual." That makes of "spirituality" one more role among many, one more attribute we use to flatter ourselves. We decide what practices, postures, and prayers are "spiritual" and what not. As if our outer life—work, pleasure, exercise, etc—weren't compartmentalized enough, we now fragment even our inner life. We turn spirituality into a spiritual disease that gnaws on our authenticity.

If someone tells you how spiritual a person he or she is, run. You're probably in the presence of a colossal fraud. Ostentatious spirituality is the very opposite of what it claims for itself. Self-proclaimed spirituality is one more facade people use to delude themselves. Real spirituality is something its practitioners live with quietly and do not use as a white cloak to cover character flaws.

Karma

Karma is a Sanskrit word that means "action." In Hindu texts it's often paired with another word, vipaka, or "result." Karma vipaka means that nothing happens without a cause. Whatever occurs does so in a larger context. All actions have consequences. Every experience conditions those that follow. All parts of life are interdependent.

Does this mean we have no freedom of choice, that things we did in the past predetermine all our decisions? Not at all. At the same time we receive the results of past action, we create new karma through our responses in the present. We can stay stuck in our old karma, repeating patterns of thought and behavior for the rest of our lives. Or we can become aware of those patterns and make the choice to break or continue them.

Part of authenticity is the exercise of our freedom. To exercise our freedom fully we require understanding of how our past actions are still affecting us. Action without insight is blind. Insight without action is impotent. Only action based on insight is free and creative. Only such action creates fresh karma. We see again the wisdom of Socrates' dictum: Know thyself. Without self-knowledge authenticity is impossible.

By action I mean not just what we do physically but also what we do mentally. One of the most powerful actions is intention. To intend, to decide on an action, is already to have taken action.

It creates karma. Authenticity means having our intentions and actions in accord. If you want someone to love you, would you beat the person until he or she did? Of course not, the intention and action conflict. This is a radical example. The sad truth is that we often behave in a way that makes of us our own adversary. Has anyone ever accused you of being your own worst enemy? Lots have me—and, I regret to admit, with good reason.

For example, I like doing things my way, being my own man, so to speak. Yet I want people to like me. Not everyone has the tolerance for radical individualism I wish they did. So my independent actions sometimes fly in the teeth of my intention to have others' acceptance, even approval.

Intention is much like attitude. Our attitudes determine not just our mental health and ability to relate in a constructive way to other people; they create karma in each of our life's situations. The intention of our actions is the one place we can influence our karma. That's why we can't afford not to be aware of our attitudes. In a very real sense, we are what we intend.

Selflessness

In the chapter "What Authenticity Is," we saw why the self is not an entity but a process. Elsewhere I discussed ways of enhancing authenticity, despite the self's elusiveness. Now let's look at how clinging to what we call our self can become an obstacle to authenticity.

A paradox of authenticity is that it requires us to create a healthy sense of self and to give up most, or all, of our ideas about what makes us a self. Our identity is ultimately a mystery to us. When we identify too strongly with our feelings, thoughts, roles, judgments, bodies, habits, ideals, perceptions, heroes, desires, or ambitions—any of the components of that little self psychologists call the ego—we remove ourselves from the realization that none of these things, alone or together, accounts for all that we are.

Authenticity demands that we look beyond these partial identities. Consoling as they are, they also cause us problems. We fear their loss. Without them, we think, we will become less real; maybe even disappear except as a corporeal shell. Yet the self we imagine, the set of ideas and descriptions we refer to as "self image," is just a picture. It's a representation, the way a painting of a sunflower is a representation and is not the flower itself. To realize our potential for authenticity, for living freely and spontaneously in the moment, we need to let go of our picture of who we are.

I like the way Robert Blanton states the case for abandoning our self-image in his book *Radical Honesty.* "Who we are is the being without any identity, within whom the mind and the perceiver and the reactor to experience reside. Who we are, is a space within which two kinds of playing occur: experience and fantasy about experience. We are not our experience, and we are not our fantasies about our experience. We are the theater in which those things occur... In order to be fully alive, we have to constantly shed attachment to ideas from the past and about the future. The biggest, fattest idea to ditch first...is the idea of who we are."

If the idea of selflessness stymies you, you're not alone. My attempts to understand it intellectually have led me in circles. "I must have a self in order to let go of my self. Does that mean the self is the 'thing' that lets its self go? What is it that is now without a self?" I just can't fathom that I can have a sense of myself (Who else is writing these words and thinking these thoughts?) and at the same time no self. What you and I and everyone can have is awareness that our carefully crafted, long-cultivated identities are both sources of comfort and spiritual chains.

Authenticity, in its spiritual aspect, is about understanding that we are both somebody and nobody. The qualities we develop and embrace help to identify us to our selves and others. They also get in our way when we fix upon them. These representations become misrepresentations. Just as the god we define is not the true God, the self we define is not the true self. The true self is not a self; it's both less and more. It is a process, a work in perpetual progress we can nurture and discover—and, yes, celebrate—through a lifetime.

The true self comes to us as one unknown, without recommendations or job descriptions, psychological attributes or emotional fanfare. It beckons us to surrender our ideas about it, leave off pursuing it, as though it were the solution to a puzzle or goal of any kind, even spiritual. Only then, now and again, sometimes when we least expect it, it may reveal its ineffable and magnificent mystery.

———————

When Souls Commune

MORE ABOUT GARY MICHAEL

Gary Michael holds M.A.'s in Philosophy and English and a Ph.D. in Humanities. He is a former radio and television announcer and actor. Gary produced and directed a television program called Easy Speak and was the subject of another one called Drawing the Nude.

The only American-born member of the National Speakers Association who has taught seminars in three foreign languages, his articles have been featured in magazines as diverse as *American Artist, Colorado Business, Professional Speaker, The Toastmaster, Palette Talk, The Georgia Review, Journal of General Education, Southwest Art,* and *The Bloomsbury Review.*

Gary's previous book, *Get In Bed With Your Audience And Satisfy Them EVERY Time,* was on the Tattered Cover's best-seller list, is the text for all speech classes at St. Mary's University of Minnesota and is in high demand by audiences across the country. He is a professional speaker in the areas of authenticity, leadership and passion management. He makes public speaking *FUN.*

His clients include Dames & Moore, Dean Witter Reynolds, the United States Air Force, Toastmasters International, Federally-Employed Women, Advanced Business Consulting, Denver Art Museum, Rotary International, the United States Department of Interior, Kenneth H. Wells & Associates, Flying Colors Art Workshops and the Colorado Dental Association. Also doctors, lawyers and politicians, including former Colorado governor Roy Romer.

Gary has climbed fifty of Colorado's fifty-four 14,000-foot peaks. He has won both city and state tennis championships. He is a compulsive dog-doter, chocolate consumer and art viewer.